Bourgueil · Musc
Brouilly · Beaune ·
tés · Collioure · Aloxe-Corton · Vouvray
· Champagne · Côte de Nuits · Chardonn
oir · Yquem · Bordelais · Château Lagran
kay · Chassagne-Montrachet · Gevrey-Ch
·Saint-Georges · Château Lafite Rothsch
abernet Sauvignon · Pinot Gris · Gamay
· Chasselas · Maury · Chablis · Pome
het · Monthélie · Vosne-Romanée · Sance
tignan · Quincy · Reuilly · Clos de Tart ·
mbertin · Châteauneuf-du-Pape · Saint-Ju
nes · Côtes du Rhône · Régnié · Bourgog
aujolais · Volnay · Saint-Estèphe · Côte
sé · Château Margaux · Pommard · Rivesa
· Saint-Amour · Romanée-Conti · Morg
ut-Brion · Pétrus · Moulin-à-Vent · Pinot N
ton Rothschild · Riesling · Sylvaner · Tok

...Julien · Banyuls · Saint-Émilion · Meur... ...rgogne · Bourgueil · Muscadet · Côtes de L... ...-de-Brouilly · Beaune · Clos Vougeot · P... ...esaltes · Collioure · Aloxe-Corton · Vouvray... ...gon · Champagne · Côte de Nuits · Chardo... ...t Noir · Yquem · Bordelais · Château Lag... ...Tokay · Chassagne-Montrachet · Gevrey-... ...uits-Saint-Georges · Château Lafite Roths... ...Cabernet Sauvignon · Pinot Gris · Gama... ...énas · Chasselas · Maury · Chablis · Po... ...rachet · Monthélie · Vosne-Romanée · Sa... ...rontignan · Quincy · Reuilly · Clos de Tar... ...Chambertin · Châteauneuf-du-Pape · Saint... ...uternes · Côtes du Rhône · Régnié · Bour... ...Beaujolais · Volnay · Saint-Estèphe · C... ...uissé · Château Margaux · Pommard · Riv... ...doc · Saint-Amour · Romanée-Conti · M... ...Haut-Brion · Pétrus · Moulin-à-Vent · Pin... ...Mouton Rothschild · Riesling · Sylvaner ·

FRENCH WINE

An Illustrated Miscellany

FRENCH WINE

An Illustrated Miscellany

Bernard Pivot
of the Académie Goncourt

Series edited by
Jean-Claude Simoën and Ghislaine Bavoillot

Plon | Flammarion

Contents

7	*Preface*: Bread and Wine	139	Languedoc-Roussillon
13	To Your (Very Good) Health!	140	The Loire Valley
16	Wines of Alsace	146	Red Wines of the Médoc
20	Wine and Love	149	Communion Wine
25	Aromas and Bouquets	154	Vintages
28	Divinities and the Vine	158	Monks and Winemaking
36	Beaujolais	166	Enologists
48	Bordeaux	171	Pétrus
55	Corked	172	Pinot Noir
56	Burgundy	175	Provence
65	Charles Bukowski	179	Grapes
68	Down in the Cellar	180	Winegrowers' Rivalry
76	Champagne	187	Romanée-Conti
85	Chardonnay	196	Saint Vincent
89	Châteauneuf-du-Pape	202	Wine and Sex
90	The Classification of 1855	211	Sommeliers
96	Blind Tasting	214	Brotherhood of the Knights of the Tasting Cup
105	God and Wine		
109	Dom Pérignon	219	Corkscrews
112	Label Art	223	Barrels
118	Haut-Brion	228	Grape-picking
123	Persian Bards	237	Veuve Clicquot
127	Drunkenness	240	Château d'Yquem
134	Krug	246	*Zinc*

Preface

Bread and Wine

My sole qualifications for compiling this *Illustrated Miscellany* are a love of wine and a childhood spent gamboling among the vines. I also have had the great good fortune to be able to enjoy wine regularly during the course of my life.

That doesn't really amount to much compared to the expertise and experience of professionals, be they winegrowers, enologists, merchants, cellarmen, sommeliers, journalists, and label experts (bearing the label "expert" themselves), or just wine buffs and buffers. But what writer born in a vineyard in a village that bears the name of an appellation would not jump at the chance to "vinify" an entire book, with words they have learned to savor, in praise of wines they have learned to write about? I may not be the best authority to do this, but I have absolutely no intention simply to go through the motions of filling a certain number of pages after having emptied a certain number of bottles. So, rather than being gripped by fear and loathing, I embarked on this book with a mixture of delight and pleasure: not only could I drink wine, I could also write about it afterward.

The present volume, it should be said, is neither a handbook for wine tasting nor a list of the foremost suppliers. In books, as in newspapers, numerous well-qualified colleagues are on hand to guide the imbibing public. It is not a comprehensive encyclopedia of vineyards, of varieties, of appellations and classifications, of vine tending and enological techniques, nor is it a universal history of vines and wines. It is not a literary and artistic anthology, nor even a political, legal, medical, or religious treatise on what is a highly controversial subject. That could occupy dozens of volumes.

Page 2 A glass of Château Lagrange, *grand cru classé* Saint-Julien Bordeaux.
Page 4 Line drawing by the French cartoonist Avoine, private collection.
Facing page Bread and wine still life by seventeenth-century Dutch painter Isaac Luttichuys.

Yet there is a little bit of all of this in my thirsty book. Still, though I am aging, if not yet "in oak" (touch wood!), I won't go so far as to say that my book could not benefit from a few more years' "laying down." The sole subject of the following pages is what I have learned, what I love, what I'm really passionate about. It contains elements of autobiography and excerpts from books I've read, as well as memories from the cellar, the fermentation room, the dining table, and the barstool; it contains portraits of wine men, women, and châteaus, of vineyards and bottles, pages on corkscrews, wine tasting, and wine bouquet—on the whole array of objects, feelings, and words that accompanied this Casanova in his endless pursuit of pretty... bottles.

For this is the essential thing: wine is part of civilization. Because we cultivate the vine, of course, but also because it is part of our spiritual culture. In an age that considers wine to be on the same level as alcohol made from corn or potatoes, this book strives to highlight the cultural dimension of a product now consumed all over the world. In the mythical as well as in the nutritional memory of man, nothing has been more essential than bread and wine. They join together at work and at rest, in effort and in pleasure, and were both present at the inaugural meal of the Christian miracle. In the history and fables of Greco-Roman antiquity, in epics (*The Iliad* and *The Odyssey*), and in sacred texts (the Bible), wine—sometimes a boon, sometimes an interdict—seems to outdo even bread itself.

The list of writers, from Homer to Colette, who have celebrated wine, or who have given it a walk-on part in their human comedies, is endless. Less perhaps than blood, less than money, but often associated with one or both, and more still with love and success, wine flows copiously at the opera house, in the theater and the movie house, as well as in painting and song. For better or for worse, since the dawn of time and until the end of the world, wine has been inextricably linked to the history of man, to his civilization, to his art, and to the unfathomable mystery of How and Why. In short: wine is no half-pint.

Winegrowers are creators: they are craftsmen and artists. The finest even sign their works, like authors. French wine is amazingly diverse. Its palette of colors, its range of flavors, is the widest in the world. I do not know them all and I fraternize with some more readily than others. A question of birth and residence, of travel and vacations, of friendship, affinity, and (of course) opportunity. But no wine ever leaves me stone cold. Those absent from this cellar book that has no cellar, from this voyage of discovery through the lands of wine, belong, let us say, to my *reserve*. It's always good to have a writer—and indeed a wine—left to discover.

The English may not produce much wine, but they have certainly had some great ideas! Hindered by their climate from becoming great winegrowers, their taste and imagination have turned them into inventors, arbiters for everything connected with imbibing. The vintages of Bordeaux, of Porto, of Madeira, among many others, owe what they are to the demands of drinkers from across the Channel. And it was essentially the noses and palates of the English that drafted the famous Bordeaux Classification of 1855.

It was not enough, though, for them to make their name in the wine trade: English industrialists and craftsmen have also contributed much to the manufacture of the bottle as we know it today. Firstly, with regard to the firing of the glass and to the adoption of the square-shouldered cylindrical bottle, known as the "Bordeaux" type. Secondly, in the mass production of corks. And, finally, in the invention of increasingly user-friendly and sophisticated corkscrews: the first patent in the world was lodged, in 1795, by a London clergyman. Perhaps some will be surprised that I write with such lightheartedness and amusement about a subject that quenches the thirst of both mouth and soul. This is only my way of taking it seriously. Wine makes me merry, so why should my ink be sour, off-putting, or cloying? There is a French expression that perfectly conveys the social role of wine in France: a *"vin d'honneur,"* a toast with wine. Who would dream of raising a glass full of water, whisky, or pastis to someone? Who would so "honor" a bottle of beer or a Bloody Mary?

This *Illustrated Miscellany* is simply a toast raised in joy: to wine!

Bernard Pivot

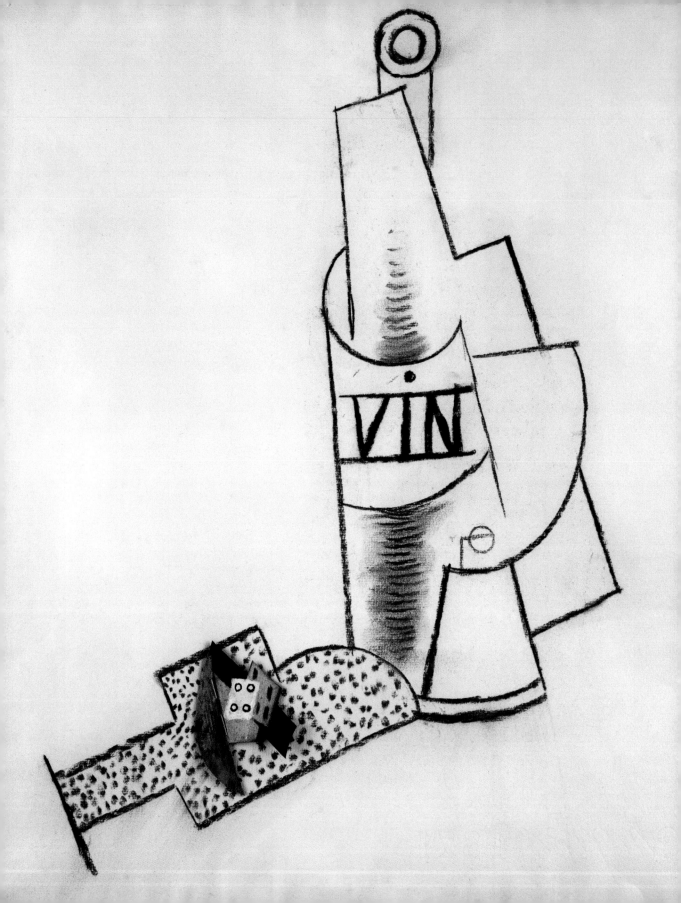

> Wine to me is passion.... It's the essence of civilization and the Art of Living.
>
> Robert Mondavi, *Harvests of Joy*

To Your (Very Good) Health!

Together, we raise a flute of champagne or a goblet of wine and we propose to drink *to* someone or something. This *"to"* is the prelude to a wish, a request, a desire. "To us!" is the most concise formulation. We are glad to meet up and have a drink together: it's time to be egoistical. Think first and foremost of "us," and wish each other all that's beautiful and good, each according to his desires. Some even cry, dispensing with the pronoun: "(Here's) to health and happiness!" One can also raise a glass for the one whose party it is, the happy cause of all this imbibing: "Your health!" "Your good health!" "Your *very* good health!" Then there's, "Here's to you," or numerous other exortations to health and happiness: "Cheers!" or "Bottoms up," for English-speakers, *"Santé!"* (Health) in France, *"Prost!"* (Cheers!) or *"Zum Wohl!"* (To Your Health) in Germany, *"L'Chaim!"* (To Life) in Israel, *"Sláinte!"* (To Your Health) in Ireland. The toasts *"Cin Cin!"* (Cheers!) in Italy and "Chin-Chin!" in English seem to have derived from *"Tsing-Tsing"* (Cantonese for Hello).

If one drinks first and foremost to someone's health, it is because alcohol helps to keep one's tail up; it's supposed to provide a fillip. Wishing for something as we clink a glass together, or just lift it to eye level, is to demonstrate our joy and friendship, to signal the hope that we will meet again soon, in fine fettle, to raise another glass.

One can also clink a glass or two to the health of absent friends, especially if the person or persons concerned have been kept away from the gathering due to illness. Births and christenings serve as pretexts for a good drink too, and some families even get the baby to partake, dabbing its lips with a drop of champagne. On April 3, 1867, Victor Hugo greeted the arrival of his grandson Georges with this note: "We drank to the health of the newborn baby." Drank what, I wonder? It would be nice to know.

My father could not remember whether a finger soaked in champagne was held to my lips at my baptism, though he did tell me that the guests were served Moët et Chandon. By coincidence we drank the same champagne at my engagement. And, twenty-five years later, my eldest daughter took up a PR post in that very house. Now that's what I call brand loyalty.

Page 10
Wine Bottle and Die, by Picasso, 1914. A work by Picasso appeared on labels of Mouton Rothschild 1973.

Facing page
Double Portrait with Wine Glass, by Marc Chagall. "Perched on the shoulders of his wife, Bella, who is wearing a white dress, the painter brandishes a glass of red wine, and seems to be saying: I'm celebrating our wedding anniversary. I drink to your health, my friends—drink to ours."
B. P.

Pages 14–15
Artists' Party at Skagen, 1888. Wine is a welcome guest at every get-together: here, gathered around the Danish painter P. S. Kroyer, the creator of the picture, it unites a community of artists living in Denmark.

The endless ritual toasts that take place during Russian and Chinese feasts don't really agree with me. Conversation is constantly interrupted and guests asked to listen to some (all too often hackneyed, occasionally absurd) pronouncement. Moreover, grain alcohols don't always go well with what's on the plate. The obligatory multiplication of tiny glasses filled with relentless alcohol resembles an attempt at voluntary group manslaughter.

On the other hand, I'm the first to lift a glass half full of some famous Bordeaux or an exceptional Burgundy served with the main course and command silence for one of the guests, myself included, to raise a toast. I feel it's a good way of greeting the wine, of attracting attention to it, of involving it in the satisfaction and, sometimes, the emotion of a collective vow; it's always a pleasure to repeat the procedure again with a late vintage when one gets to the dessert.

Once upon a time, in newspaper offices journalists drank at least as much as they wrote. Anything and everything could serve as a pretext for a tipple, in particular with the subs or printers. The calendar of holidays and birthdays was scrupulously observed.

Gaining a scoop, someone returning from an assignment abroad or being promoted, the publication of a book, even a departure on vacation: all these events were a signal to crack open a bottle of pastis, whisky, or wine, and known as *"Alas,"* a word derived from the first words of a French drinking song: *"A la santé du confrère / Qui nous régale aujourd'hui"* ("To the health of the colleague we're honoring today").

On June 19, 1974, when I left my job at the Paris-based daily newspaper *Le Figaro*, an announcement was posted on every door in the famous building on the Champs-Élysées intersection: "The Beaujolais will flow in abundance this Wednesday, June 19, between 5.30 and 7.30 p.m., in the office of the book pages on the occasion of Bernard Pivot's departure." Printed in tiny characters at the bottom of the notice, one could read the following: "If you have to leave, do not be afraid of the dryness of your own path, fear rather the thirst for those who remain." Confucius, *Analects*.

To me, Confucius seems far too much of a sobersides to have written that.

Wines of Alsace

France would have been right to fight to keep Alsace for no more than its Riesling, its sauerkraut, and its quetsch plum tart. Well, for good measure one might throw in Strasbourg Cathedral, Grünewald's Issenheim altarpiece, and the Humanist Library at Sélestat, as well as hundreds of splendid winegrowers' manors of the fifteenth and sixteenth centuries that have made famous villages like Colmar, Riquewihr, Ribeauvillé, Eguisheim, Obernai, and others on the wine trail.

In fact, at that time in Sélestat there lived an intellectual (the word used at the time was "humanist") by the name of Beatus Rhenanus (1485–1547); he had such a great reputation that Erasmus himself visited and befriended him. The universal philosopher of Rotterdam was so astonished that this little town in Alsace had produced so many "men distinguished in qualities of the mind" that he wrote and published a text entitled *In Praise of Sélestat*, in which he also lauds its "fertile plain" and "vine-clad slopes." By this time wine was already instrumental in the region's considerable wealth. Subsequently entering a steep decline, however, Alsace only recovered its prosperity during the second half of the twentieth century.

Like a delicious mackerel, Alsace is synonymous with white wine. It flows through its language, its grammar, its culture. Nothing more honest, more straightforward than Alsace can be imagined: its growths, for instance, simply bear the names of the grapevine varieties. Budding enologists are thus best off starting with Alsace. Beside that Rhenish prince of grapes, Riesling, which produces the most sought-after dry and floral vintages, Alsace can call on Sylvaner, Tokay (now called Pinot Gris), Pinot Blanc, the Alsace Muscat, Chasselas, and the unctuous Gewürztraminer. Mainly with the Riesling and Gewürztraminer, they obtain—when the season is suitably long and sun-drenched, which is not as rare as all that in these regions—"late-harvested grapes," or even "selections of noble grapes," that are irresistibly mellow. My favorite, late-harvest Riesling overflows with contradictions, since it keeps the stony dryness and light, flowery tones from its vine type, to which "noble rot" (what a sonorous oxymoron that is) adds a sweeter, voluptuous exuberance. The Riesling that it continues

Facing page
A bunch of Riesling grapes, the prince of Alsatian vine varieties, at the root of some of the very finest vintages.

Pages 18–19
The vines of Riquewihr grow on steep scarps that run down to the picturesque medieval city, one of the most charming in all Alsace.

to be seems almost to wrestle on the palate with the Riesling it has since become. The final variety in Alsace, the Pinot Noir, is the only one to give rosé and red wines. The rosé, like so many others, I'm not overly keen on. The red, though, is good quaffing wine. Transparent, as if diluted, it lacks body, but often hints at a healthy whiff of cherry and is fine and dandy when lightly chilled.

We were dining at Haeberlin's, at the Auberge de l'Ill. After a most endearing *grand cru* Geisberg 1998, a Ribeauvillé Riesling, Serge Dubs (voted best sommelier in the world in 1989) asked us what red we'd like to go on to. A Burgundy? A Bordeaux? I answered that I'd prefer to stay in Alsace. "Leave it to me!" he said. He returned with a bottle that turned out worthy of the best growths of Côte de Nuits: a Pinot Noir (do readers need reminding that this is the variety used for Burgundy reds?) marked with the year 1990, a "Les Neveux" (meaning The Nephews) from Hugel of Riquewihr. A dark, deep, red wine of redoubtable alcohol content (14.5 percent) and aroma, a far cry from so many run-of-the-mill, runny Pinot Noirs of Alsace. The story behind the name "The Nephews" goes like this. The Hugels have been winegrowers in Riquewihr since the mid-seventeenth century. Jean Hugel is one of the enlightened professionals who, in the wake of efforts in other great wine-producing regions, worked on the classification and regulation of Alsace wines in 1983 and 1992.

One day, his nephews told him to his face that the Pinot Noirs were simply not up to scratch, way below the standard of the vines for the whites, and that something had to be done. He told them to give it a whirl. In 1990, a year that turned out to be particularly sunny, on a well-exposed plot planted with old stocks of Pinot Noir that the nephews limited to thirty hectoliters per hectare, they vinified and aged in oak barrels what fermented into an extraordinary wine. Flabbergasted, Jean Hugel baptized the vintage "The Nephews" and they went on to renew the experience successfully with a series of generous vintages.

Other Alsatian winegrowers have produced some superb vintages with Pinot Noir. René Muré, in Rouffach, for one, with a Clos Saint-Lancelin 1999 that I tasted at the Rendez-Vous de Chasse, in Colmar. And then there's Zind-Humbrecht. But, since every business needs to turn a profit, such wines are bound to remain few and far between.

Alsace only truly triumphs under a white flag.

Wine and Love

Two French villages are lucky enough to be called Saint-Amour. The first, in the Jura, produces a Côte-de-Jura. One of its denizens was Léon Werth, a friend of Antoine de Saint-Exupéry and to whom *The Little Prince* was dedicated. The other, which bequeathed its name to one of the ten *crus* of the Beaujolais, occupies the northernmost region on the border of the Mâconnais. Less structured and luxuriant than its neighbors Moulin-à-Vent, Juliénas, and Chénas, Saint-Amour remains generally more supple and round. One needs to drink it young. If it's dubbed a *vin galant* (a lively wine), this is surely due to overspill from its magical name. It was not, however, the bright idea of some marketing director; it is said that it was here that a passing Roman legionnaire fell for a lass for whom he ditched Julius Caesar.

On St. Valentine's Day, lovers gaze into one another's eyes and down goodly quantities of Saint-Amour. Pointing to it on the menu at the beginning of a dinner for two already amounts to a declaration. The same goes for Switzerland if, on February 14, you plump for a Valentine, a Chardonnay, Pinot Noir, or Chasselas Neuchâtel. More original, but also much more expensive, if you really want to have your wicked way through your knowledge of the wine list, order a bottle of Chambolle-Musigny, *premier cru*, "Les Amoureuses."

But the wine that most frequently accompanies the words and the acts of love is, without question, champagne. Still, sometimes one hears people say of a red that it is *"amoureux"* (loving). The term cannot be applied to virile, strapping vintages, but to more delicate, tender, feminine wines. Volnay, for example, is just such a *vin amoureux*. When someone is head over heels in love and drinks in the company of the loved one, heart and wine play in unison.

And later, when love disintegrates into indifference or acrimony? Lack of affection does not lead to temperance—quite the contrary. The difference between a wine lover who is happy and in love and one not so blessed is that the latter, having no one to share in his pleasure, can go off the rails and start drinking garbage. Nursing a solitary glass, an inconsolable widower, or a man jilted and numb with pain, is not a good judge of the quality of a vintage.

Facing page
Couple at the Quatre-Saisons Bal Musette, Rue de Lappe, Paris, photographed by Brassaï, c. 1932.

Left
The Alliance between Love and Wine, Jean-Marc Nattier, 1744. "A boy sporting a plume throws a languid glance at a young woman, one of whose breasts is already peeking out. Their left hands intertwine, while she, an iota less impatient than him, stretches out an empty glass so he might pour her some wine from the carafe. The name of the vintage is not recorded. It must have been a very 'loving,' 'caressing' appellation. Was it perhaps the same one Jean-Marc Nattier was drinking when painting this masterpiece of gallantry?" B. P.

Aromas and Bouquets

Putting to one side the linguistic hogwash adopted by certain specialists, it has to be conceded that fine wines—which are, after all, simply the sum of the influence of grape variety, soil, climate, wine-making expertise, blending (for some), pressing, fermentation, and aging—exhale an extraordinary variety of bouquets. A thousand aromatic molecules, divided into half a dozen families (flowers, fruits, plants, spices, minerals, animals, etc.), have been discovered by chemists since the 1950s, captured and identified by a complicated process called chromatography. These scents are all the more extraordinary in that some molecules amount to little more than traces.

All good wines resemble more or less complicated puzzles. This is why wine-tasting—from the smell-sensitive mucous membrane of the nose all the way to the brain's olfactory memory—is a science for professionals and a game for amateurs, and for everyone an enthralling ID parade. If it is child's play to locate the red fruits of a Gamay, the spice of a Tokay, the chocolate notes of a Maury, the exotic fruit of a Gewürztraminer, the quince of Vouvray, etc., the majority of wines wear their heart less on their sleeve. One needs an excellent sense of smell and taste, as well as concentration, perceptiveness, memory, experience, and a wealth of knowledge. To really get a handle on a taste one has to be part gourmet, part gumshoe.

The catalog of wine flavors is impressive: from currant to tobacco, from bilberry to truffle, from freshly mown grass to English candies. More from humor, I suppose, than from dearth of vocabulary, some have distinguished still more surprising notes, like "baked potato," orchid, bonfire, and (the horror, the horror!) sun cream or damp shoelace. Since wine is such a bag of tricks, and of poetry, I am particularly looking forward to one day detecting in my glass that highly characteristic and sought-after aroma of the skin on an amorous young woman's neck in the Parc de Bagatelle as the sun is setting one May evening after some early rain.

Facing page
The liqueur-like wines of Sauternes (here, a glass of Yquem) develop savors of candied fruits, caramel, honey, and muscatel. This incredible aromatic palette can still be felt in older vintages.

In victory, you
deserve champagne,
in defeat you need it.

Napoleon Bonaparte

Divinities and the Vine

The Dionysus of the Greeks and the Bacchus of the Romans are one and the same divinity. If the first has the advantage of seniority and the prestige of mythological origin, on his Latin counterpart's side there are centuries of undimmed popularity among Western artists and poets.

Today Bacchus is identified as the god of the grape harvest, of wine and intoxication. This is what public opinion has reduced him to; whereas in Antiquity he was thought to have a beneficial effect on *all* agriculture. Not satisfied with merely slaking our thirst with wine, he nourished us too. At the beginning, he appeared young and handsome, with the charm that an open heart and an open hand bring. But, as he drank a lot (or, at least, was given a lot to drink), he grew flabby, his buttocks and belly bloated, love-handles appeared, and he waxed rubicund. As merry as ever, between two drinking bouts he would slouch on a throne with a crown of vine fronds on his head and a wine cup in his hand, surrounded by bacchantes. Or else he would flop astride a barrel.

Dionysus is a far more complex god than Bacchus. Of devastating beauty, his anger toward those imprudent enough to reject or even doubt his divine authority was relentless. First driving them mad, he would then destroy them. As a god of fertility, fruitfulness, and happiness, the vine—which he created, introducing it to Greece, throughout the Middle East, and to Italy and Spain—was naturally one of his specialties. Dionysus was a conqueror, a tyrant, and a benefactor of humanity all rolled into one.

Much of his pathological need for recognition is explained by his troubled birth. Son of the illicit loves of Zeus and the beautiful but all too mortal Semele, he was a mere fetus when his mother was reduced to cinders. To forestall the murderous jealousy of Hera, Zeus's missus, the god grabbed the unborn infant and sewed him into his thigh, where he completed his development. Indeed, so well protected was the child Dionysus by Silenus (his tutor and a marvelously talented drunkard), assisted by assorted nymphs, maenads, and satyrs, that the queen of the gods never managed to get her talons into him. Then, escaping killers hired by his mother-in-law, Dionysus traveled the world proclaiming his divine nature and the extraordinary capacities he had inherited

Page 26
The quality of the harvest depends on winter pruning. A vineyard under the snow in Languedoc-Roussillon.

Facing page
Hardly more than a teenager, Caravaggio's *Bacchus* (c. 1595) holds out a cup of wine to visitors to the Uffizi in Florence.

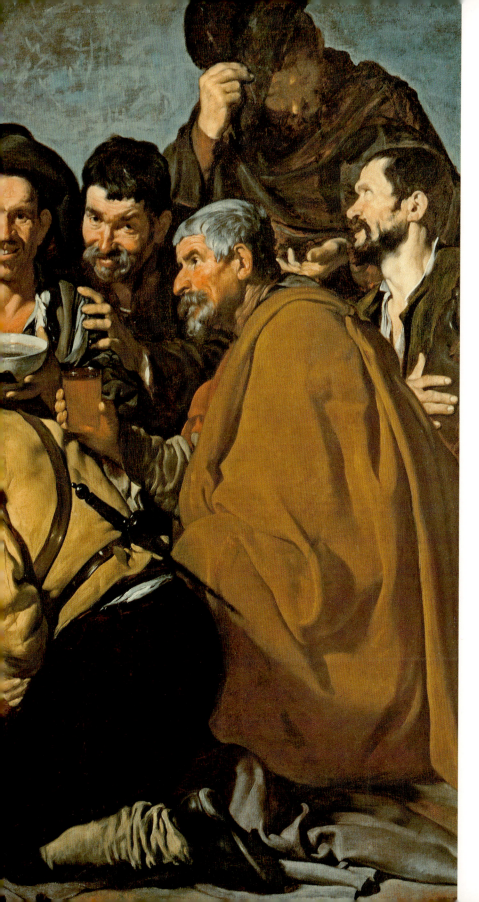

Left
A young Bacchus refreshes and inebriates seven worthy drinkers in this picture by Velázquez (c. 1628).

Facing page
The Autumn fountain in the park at the Château of Versailles. The Bacchus, made of gilded lead, symbolizes the season of the grape harvest.

from his father. What better gift could he make to humanity than the vine and wine?

Bacchus and Venus are the only gods whom uncharitable Christianity seems to have spared during its cleanup of Mount Olympus. Their rescue from oblivion is due to the popularity of their respective areas of expertise: wine and love. Under their Greek names of Dionysus and Aphrodite, and after a meal washed down with copious drafts of the better wines from the island of Chios, they inevitably fell into bed, giving rise to Priapus, a sex maniac with disproportionate attributes.

Venus owes an immense debt to the great painters of the Renaissance. Luckily, they could celebrate her beauty with all the more sensuality, since here was a woman who could be depicted nude without shocking the Church (overmuch). She was after all only a wanton, pretty pagan, and thus a shameless hussy!

Bacchus's pictorial roll call is almost as impressive as that of his divine one-night stand. If Bellini's plump child oozes charm, the youthful beauty of Michelangelo's bronze is striking. He hasn't yet had a drink. Imbibing with a serious air, Caravaggio's Bacchus, his head girded in vine leaves and a cup half filled with red wine in his left hand, has just emerged from adolescence. Bare-chested, the still young Bacchus of Velázquez seems to have taken leave of his senses. Seated on a cask, he crowns a drunkard kneeling in front of him, while others no less pickled watch on. Leonardo's version oddly resembles a St. John the Baptist, surprised on the road from water to wine. Rubens, with his taste for bulky flesh, paints a rotund Bacchus who long ago bid farewell to his feet, as a decadent, nightmarish pasha.

In folk art, Bacchus even outdoes the goddess of love. In porcelain, earthenware, plaster, wood, even chocolate, the vinous god pops up all over the place. Associated with moral relativism, the name of Dionysus coalesced into a hedonistic philosophy (represented yesterday by Nietzsche and today by Michel Onfray), producing poetry in praise of wine, intoxication, license, and impious vice. Accompanied by a whole theory of liberty, disorder, and secrecy, his triumph in the form of his Latin moniker has been popularized by derivations from his name: bacchanal (a noisy and wine-soaked orgy), bacchic or bacchanalian (songs, brotherhoods, feasts, etc.).

Bacchus, dear and antediluvian companion of the binge, we who are about to drink salute you!

God only made water
But man made wine.

Victor Hugo, *La fête chez Thérèse*

Facing page *Bacchus, Venus, and Love*, by Rosso Fiorentino (c. 1531): a masterpiece from the collection of the Musée National d'Histoire et d'Art in Luxembourg.

Beaujolais

As a presenter of a TV literary program called *Apostrophes*, my Beaujolais origins were often cited as a drawback. Surely a contradiction must lurk between great literature and a wine swilled by *boules* players? Could one rely on an imbiber of such a tipple to chair a discussion with Marcel Jouhandeau, Georges Dumézil, Marguerite Yourcenar, Claude Lévi-Strauss, Julien Green, or some other luminary of the French intellectual scene? My fondness for soccer didn't go down too well either, and some intellectuals, of both rightist and leftist persuasion, as well as the occasional colleague, seriously wondered if there wasn't an element of play-acting in the fact that I appeared to have a certain taste in books, while I palpably had none when it came to drink. In short, is Proust soluble in a glass of Beaujolais? A Médoc *premier cru* or a vintage champagne is admittedly a superior accompaniment—the point is hardly arguable—when reading *In Search of Lost Time*. But the contrast between a rough-and-ready wine and a distinguished work of fiction may raise a smile, and anyhow I drank and enjoyed many other wines—in point of fact, Médocs and champagne as well. In this squabble over my qualities as a professional reader, which was predicated on my viticultural origins, I will not go so far as to claim racism (such a serious word should be left to those who suffer from it seriously), but winery intolerance there indubitably was.

Had I been born and raised among the châteaus of Bordeaux or the houses of Champagne, I would never have been teased about the drink of my fledgling years in this fashion. Wines from elsewhere don't spawn the same stories because they are rare or discreet—like the Mondeuse of Savoy or the Sciaccarello of Corsica; or historic—like Jurançon or Chinon; or mellow—like Bonnezeaux or Sauternes; or arty, like Château Ausone or Côtes-de-Duras. But Beaujolais is none of these things: it is a wine of the people. I imagine that, in the eyes of certain bookworms and/or cellar rats in the Sorbonne and the French Institute, this meant I should have been confined to reviewing best sellers. Still, it would be wrong of me to peel off the Beaujolais label stuck over my ID card. I think it grew to form part and parcel of an image (reassuring to the majority of viewers) of a journalist, who, at table,

was one of them, and who didn't change when he walked on set and chatted to his guests.

The charm of Beaujolais country is something everyone can agree on: these are some fine-looking vineyards. Undulating hills and meandering valleys compose a "typically French" landscape, with temperate summers, with sudden glimpses of space and dreamy digressions, while an upland forest plays in the background. With its splendid villages of golden stone, the southern Beaujolais—also known as the Bas Beaujolais—is more touristy than the north, but, the farther one moves away from Lyon, and the closer one gets to Mâcon, the better the wine. Crudely: in the south, plain and simple Beaujolais, in the center Beaujolais-Villages, and to the north, the majority of the better growths.

Unanimity is also to be found with regards to the friendliness and joviality of the local winegrowers. Here hospitality has been honed to a fine art. This oils the wheels of commerce, of course, but the inhabitants are naturally convivial and, without fuss or ceremony, enjoy clinking a glass or two. Unpretentious, clubbable, the very word "Beaujolais" sounds almost gaudy. In its genius the French vernacular—perhaps two sheets to the wind and thus inspired, and aided and abetted by a potboiling author or two—has coined words to describe its produce such as *beaujo, beaujolo, beaujol, beaujolpif,* all conveying the hail-fellow-well-met cordiality of the winemakers and the rugged (good) humor of the consumers.

But just let "Beaujolais" refer to the actual *wine* and not to the region or the appellation's home patch, and one stirs up a hornet's nest buzzing with misplaced prejudice and deserved reproach. Let's take a closer look.

Is Beaujolais a newfangled wine? While it is one of the least ancient French wine regions, Beaujolais (it takes its name from the historical capital, Beaujeu) has been in the viticulture game for donkey's years. At least since the tenth century, the date of a charter from Mâcon that attests to its presence. It is true, though, that the region has always had more than one string to its agricultural bow. The rye fields and meadows were more numerous and of larger size than the vineyards, which only began to proliferate and gobble up land from the mid-eighteenth century and then in the nineteenth, and more still after World War II. The region nevertheless produced enough wine—of a good enough

Pages 36–37
"Observations of the Beaujolais, impressions of the Beaujolais, daydreams of the Beaujolais… hands from the Beaujolais."
B. P.
The cover of *Beaujolaises,* by Bernard Pivot, with photographs by Pierre Cottin.

Facing page
"I had a particular liking for those winemakers whose mustache would quiver just above the shiny round metal top of the tasting cup." B. P.

Pages 40–41
"Jacques Gruber is a master glassmaker from the School of Nancy. He is the creator of the glass canopy above the Galeries Lafayette, among others. I was delighted to be able to purchase a picture by him at auction called *Autumn* that I'm always glad to see again when I get back to my house in the Beaujolais." B. P.

quality—for Voltaire to have chosen it as his everyday tipple at home in Ferney.

Is Beaujolais a Burgundy? Historically and geographically speaking—Beaune is 125 kilometers from Villefranche-sur-Saône, the administrative capital of the Beaujolais region—Burgundy and Beaujolais have nothing to do with one another. And as to vine and wine, they are chalk and cheese. The scarps of Burgundy are planted essentially with Chardonnay and Pinot Noir, while the slopes of the Beaujolais are dedicated to Gamay Noir, giving white juice. Lastly, to the nose and palate, a red Burgundy is a far cry from Beaujolais *rouge*. They are not vinified in the same manner. One can survive to a ripe old age; the other perishes young. In terms of quality and reputation, their status is very different. And yet, since an edict dated 1930, in wine terms, Beaujolais "belongs" to Burgundy. With the result that the latter now stretches from Auxerre and its Chablis to Villefranche and its Beaujolais. The administration has unified and simplified, though this does not authorize a Beaujolais to claim to be a Burgundy (and neither would a Burgundy exercise its humility to the point of wanting to pass for a Beaujolais). A number of exceptions, as ever, prove the rule: flying in the face of any logic, the ten growths of Beaujolais (Brouilly, Côte-de-Brouilly, Chénas, Chiroubles, Fleurie, Juliénas, Morgon, Moulin-à-Vent, Régnié, Saint-Amour) have earned the right, indeed the honor, to emblazon "Burgundy" on their labels. In truth, only one should be admitted: Moulin-à-Vent. In effect, grown in an exceptional year and suitably aged, due to the manganese in the soil, a strange alchemy renders its Gamay more like a Pinot. "Burgundyized" in this fashion, after at least five years aging, at a blind tasting it can be confused with something from the *climat* (area) of Côte de Nuits.

Has Beaujolais become a victim of its own success? Yes, and in more ways than one, since its very popularity, as is all too evident, gets up the noses of a lot of people, maybe because it has got too big for its boots. In the heady years of yore, its producers' federation lacked a leader with the perspicacity, foresight, guts, and muscle to prevent vines being dotted about in absurd numbers on chilly, poorly exposed uplands, or in the cereal-growing valleys of the Bas Beaujolais. He might too have suggested to winegrowers of his Comité Interprofessionnel that they moderate the use of weedkillers and manure. He would have fought against overproduction. And he would have condemned *surchaptalisation* (basically, adding too much sugar). He would have understood that rigor and quality are the only guarantors of enduring success and that they have to be fostered—enforced, even.

Has the Beaujolais Nouveau arrived yet? Scholar and historian Gilbert Garrier had little trouble proving that "the great expectation for new wine" has always existed, even in ancient Rome. Since imitated by other wines, "Beaujolais Primeur" is simply the most recent and most spectacular illustration, since the Gamay grape, following a brief stint in the fermentation vat, reveals its red fruit flavor in a flash.

In the 1950s this "new" Beaujolais was a rather esoteric product. Demand was greater among Paris café owners than the winegrowers could meet. In everyone's interest, production gradually snowballed: a novel pleasure for some, it meant a fast buck for others. According to Garrier, it was not before 1975—a poor year, but it was at this time that the enthusiasm overflowed from the barrel—that the fad for early *primeur* conquered all Paris, when the publication of René Fallet's novel, *Le beaujolais nouveau est arrivé* (The Beaujolais Nouveau has arrived), coincided with the official baptism of the newborn at a French National Assembly presided over by Edgar Faure, and the publicity afforded it by singers Georges Brassens and Mireille Mathieu.

And from Paris, Beaujolais Nouveau struck out to conquer our European neighbors and, in the end, the entire globe. By chance I have been present at its disembarkation both in Montreal and Bamako. In Canada, in spite of the cold, it was a day of indescribable jubilation in bars and restaurants. By midnight, every bottle had been drunk. In Mali, the French, European, and American communities greeted it in evening dress, on the occasion of a very chic banquet held beneath the mango trees and eucalypti on the banks of the River Niger.

The meteoric rise of Beaujolais Nouveau is a psychological rather than enological phenomenon. November is the drabbest month of the year. Bleak, dank, blustery. Christmas feels a long way off. The tedium. Everyone feels down in the dumps. And it is then that, on the third Thursday of the month, there bowls in a merry, bold wine with ruddy cheeks, bringing a taste of spring to the mouth; a drink to be guzzled rather than sipped, like an elixir

Below
Bernard Pivot in his family's village of Quincié-en-Beaujolais: "This is where I learned to appreciate, to love wine." B. P.

Above
"Beaujolais Nouveau is not a *premier cru*: it's Beaujolais Nouveau, and that's that. It's a cheeky little plonk, a scamp of a wine, a fun but poetical thingamajig," René Fallet.

Pages 44–45
All the charm of the Beaujolais landscape: the village of Villié-Morgon nestling within the vineyards of Morgon.

of youth and gaiety. In such autumnal melancholy, a common desire for partying finds its expression in the arrival of a "new" wine. It's simply lucky enough to turn up at the right time.

Still, if fashion certainly had a hand in launching the vogue for Beaujolais Nouveau, the tide seems to have turned now. The wine has undergone the fate of writers who are scorned or lambasted by the same critics who, having flattered them in their early days, now can't bear to see them camped out at the top of the best-seller lists. There are of course good and less good years (yet it is not the most sun-drenched harvest or the musts with the highest alcohol content that conspire to make the best Beaujolais Nouveau): each November has its own batch of bottles—excellent, pleasant, or, alas, nondescript, revolting, even. But I can testify to the fact that, generally speaking, the wine has been rather better in recent times than it was twenty or thirty years back.

This change is inevitable: customers and tastes vary. The wait is no longer so innocent, nor so forgiving. The general public, especially in Paris, has gradually been convinced by enologists, wine waiters, and sundry journalists, aggrieved at the yearly fad for the uppity wine, that the fame enjoyed by this fresh-faced star amounts to an injustice. These high-principled fellows insist that the success of a wine should be in exact proportion to its excellence, to its aging capacity, to its scarcity. Beaujolais Nouveau is a glaring exception to such a moral conception of the world. But it may be a rascal, an imp, a good-for-nothing, a rude-boy, a wide-boy, even—but a swindler: never! The truth is that it is a hard wine to like once one is no longer in the party mood. Fun isn't what it used to be; perhaps because the Beaujolais Nouveau (40 percent of the harvest) undermines traditional Beaujolais and the vintages that spend winter quietly maturing in the cellar. It eclipses what is yet to come: the best. For many consumers, Beaujolais just means Beaujolais Nouveau. And when they discover a long line of other appellations standing behind it, like a benefactor at a charity dinner, they wave them away: "I've already donated." Thus, the more Beaujolais Nouveau made inroads, the harder the others found it to make their way.

I raise my glass—I say, it contains Régnié!—to the man or woman who manages to extricate Beaujolais from this philosophic and economic quandary.

What contemptible scoundrel
stole the cork from my lunch?

**W. C. Fields as Larson E. Whipsnade
in *You Can't Cheat an Honest Man* (1939)**

Facing page   The Bottle of Bordeaux, Georges Rohner, 1968.
This artist often chose the theme of a laid table for his still lifes.

Bordeaux

No one likes the English, Irish, and Americans more than people from the Bordeaux region. The names of the brokers, traders, and owners who arrived by ship testify to some successful social integration: Lawton, Barton, Johnston, Brown, McCarthy, Maxwell, Palmer, Lynch, Colck, Lichine, Mitchell, etc., not forgetting the British offshoot of the Rothschilds. It is also through the port, or airport, of Bordeaux that the countless British and US writers and journalists who have written on French wines enter the country: Richard Olney, William Echikson, Oz Clarke, Margaret Rand, James Turnbull, Robert Parker, David Cobbold, Dewey Markham, Hugh Johnson, Nicholas Faith, Kermit Lynch, Andrew Jefford, Tom Stevenson. Even with its omissions, that's some impressive list.

The Dutch were similarly well received. Beyerman, their oldest wine-merchant house, was founded in Bordeaux in 1620. It was a Hollander who invented a modern, fail-safe way of decanting from one barrel to another (racking). "The first barrel has to be disinfected and the Dutchmen found that by burning wicks of sulfur one might thoroughly eliminate bacteria from the barrel. When I was a child, these sulfur wicks were still called Dutch matches." And who is our informant? A merchant from Les Chartrons, of an unimpeachably Bordelais background, the late Hugues Lawton.

In this context, it comes as little surprise that, in *L'Amateur de Bordeaux* (The Lover of Bordeaux), Jean-Robert Pitte judiciously wondered whether wine from Bordeaux wasn't a touch Protestant? Rather more so, if you like, than dyed-in-the-wool Catholic Burgundy and champagne. The Protestant periodical *Réforme* applauded, while apostolic geographers of Bordeaux, Jean-Robert Pitte's colleagues, ground their teeth. Part of this "nobility of the cork" is, however, indeed Protestant. It seems to me that, in the mouth, a Médoc, much more than a Pomerol or Saint-Émilion, does possess an immediately austere complexity, feeling a scintilla Anglican (I do not say Calvinist) under the tooth, stemming from the tannins that long meditate so as to plump up the wine and allow its soul to commune in all its richness. Catholics are in a greater hurry. Bernard Frank based his religion on the fact: "Before I'd even sniffed a Bordeaux, as a child, it was the Protestant, the persecuted, the Armagnac, the English who made

Facing page
Château Margaux, one of the most majestic in the Médoc.

Pages 50–51
At Lafite Rothschild, in the wine storehouse designed by Ricardo Bofill, the barrels are arranged like spokes around the imposing rotunda.

Pages 52–53
In the fog of twilight, the gate to Château Canon seems to keep guard over the vines of this *premier grand cru classé* in Saint-Émilion.

me love it. Burgundy was for me the dreadful Catholic and the Bavarian, all the burden of the world" (*Vingt ans avant* [Twenty years before]).

In the Bordeaux region, châteaus are as common as swimming pools in Hollywood: they're everywhere. Except that not all of these châteaus are, from an architectural point of view, "country seats." A few hectares of vine are enough to raise a house to the nobility, to give it a past, luster. It's not the château that plants the vine; it's from the vine that sprouts the château. This is the only wine-producing region in the world where the vine confers on its owner the eminent social advantage of affixing their name to a "château"—even if they actually live in a bungalow or a downtown apartment. In a bottle of Bordeaux, one buys and drinks architecture.

Joking apart, the authentic châteaus and noble residences are often splendid, in particular in the Graves and the Médoc. A Gironde vineyard looks so gorgeous, so prosperous, that it gives the impression of always having lived the high life. Yet that's wrong too, because Bordeaux, no less than other wine-producing regions, was laid waste by the scourge of phylloxera. It was hit harder by the two world wars than the others because it depended so much on international trade and transport. Between these two conflicts, the Wall Street Crash brought more than one estate to its knees. Lastly, during the record-breaking freeze of 1956, even the pluckiest were on the verge of throwing in the towel. Since then, thankfully, the situation has improved. And a lot, especially for the classified vintages, the *crus classés*. Because the recent downturn (which has to do with world wine overproduction, as well as—in the Bordeaux region and elsewhere—with the unthinking extension of vines planted and awarded appellation status) has only seriously affected "Bordeaux Supérieurs" and the run-of-the-mill red and white Bordeaux, spilling over onto wines classified just above in the hierarchy. The dazzling affluence of châteaus in the Médoc, Pomerol, and Saint-Émilion contrasts with the hardship felt in common-or-garden domains.

Be that as it may. Through its history, by the variety and quality of its wines, by the sumptuousness of the very finest, by its vast extent, by its situation on the shores of the ocean facing the New World, by its prestige and cultural cachet, Bordeaux has to be regarded as the premier wine region on the planet.

Corked

In a restaurant, whenever a wine betrays the telltale signs of being "corked," you send back the bottle. At home, you would have already taken care to test the wine, and, if it had the abominable, the hateful, the pitiless taste of "cork," you'd have binned it.

Actually, wines have many ways of being corked. They differ according to the type of stopper, the length of time the contents have been afflicted, the nature of the wine, and on how the curse develops once the wine is left to breathe. Some "cork-like" odors, perceptible as soon as the bottle is opened, vanish in a few minutes. But such a miracle does not always occur.

Sometimes, between courtesy and a corked wine, one is obliged to plump, for courtesy's sake, for an act that entails drinking (a little) of the said corked wine. This happened with ex-Chancellor Helmut Kohl, whom I once asked for an interview. My request granted, a TV crew from France 2 and I traveled hotfoot to Bonn. Very hail-fellow-well-met, Helmut Kohl expiated at length to camera on German cuisine and wines that he said he preferred to beer. At the end, he invited the whole crew over to his vast office for a tot of Riesling.

The maître d' naturally started by pouring a glass for the chancellor, who, having tasted it, gave the nod for a general round. This Riesling, however, was not just corked. It was (to recall the improper if devastating expression I whispered under my breath at the time) "corked to the bone."

If someone had offered me a wine like that to sample, I'd have suggested that it had been the innocent victim of pentachlorophenol or of some other contamination with no respect for borders. But how could anyone voice the opinion that the Riesling was plainly undrinkable, without undermining, embarrassing, humiliating even, Herr Kohl? Excluding the unlikely hypothesis that he simply hadn't detected the taste of the cork, there are only a few explanations for the statesman's attitude. Perhaps he tasted the wine too quickly, perceiving his error only after his guests had started to drink and thus too late to call it back. Or perhaps he knew there was no more wine in the office fridge. Or perhaps he was relying on our lack of taste or of courage.

Facing page
Once he has drawn the cork from the bottle, the wine waiter lifts it to his nose to check whether there's no olfactory sign that the wine might be spoiled (*Sniffing the Cork*, an illustration by Charles Martin).

Burgundy

Besides Chablis, Mâconnais, and Beaujolais—which are but grand dependences, beautiful annexes—historic Burgundy, true Burgundy, is not a very extensive region. Three Côtes: de Nuits, de Beaune, and de Chalon occupy about 9,000 hectares (22,240 acres), that is to say roughly half that of Beaujolais, around one-thirteenth of Bordeaux: Bordeaux occupies 296,500 acres (120,000 hectares). Greater Burgundy extends only to 98,840 acres (40,000 hectares), satellites included. Of modest size but immense in prestige, historic Burgundy presents the best "surface-area-to-fame" ratio of any wine-producing region in the world.

For a foreigner, to learn the French wine map is a piece of cake. Isn't it? In Alsace, the reader can just memorize grapevine varieties, in Champagne, the brands or *marques*, in Bordeaux, the châteaus. And in Burgundy, the villages. And what villages! Their names have been aged, labeled, *chambré*, and tasted for centuries. But Meursault, Chassagne-Montrachet, Puligny-Montrachet, Volnay, Pommard, Monthélie, Gevrey-Chambertin, Nuits-Saint-Georges, Vougeot, Vosne-Romanée, Chambolle-Musigny, etc., are only tiny hamlets, some with fewer than five hundred inhabitants. And yet many are better known on every continent than capitals such as Ashgabat, Windhoek, Asmara, and Tallinn. As for Beaune, it's practically Alexandria! Today, as in former times, Burgundy possesses the reputation of being the most accessible and the least strait-laced wine region in France. Alsace is good too, but it cheats with its beer. There is still something medieval, Bacchic, noisily festive about Burgundy's image and the reputation of the Burgundians, starting with the famous ritual round of applause in which one waves one's hands to the tune of *la-la-la-la-la-la-la-lalère* and claps in time. Indeed no other wine region has been the source of so many popular songs: "Happy Children of Burgundy," "Another L'il Glass of Wine," "We Plant the Vines," "Let's Go Harvesting," and many more.

The Burgundian appetite is legendary. The inhabitants are strapping fellows who like their food, enjoy a bit of fun; they are men of the soil, of the *terroir*, who do their duty. However, the traditional image of Burgundy and its denizens is becoming less and less accurate. It is kept alive for folklore, wheeled out for days

Facing page
A historic poster for French railroads featuring some of Burgundy's top sites: Beaune and its hospices, Dijon, and the wines.

Pages 58–59
A vineyard in Chassagne-Montrachet. A *grand cru* from the Côte de Beaune in Côte-d'Or, it is the most famous Burgundy white.

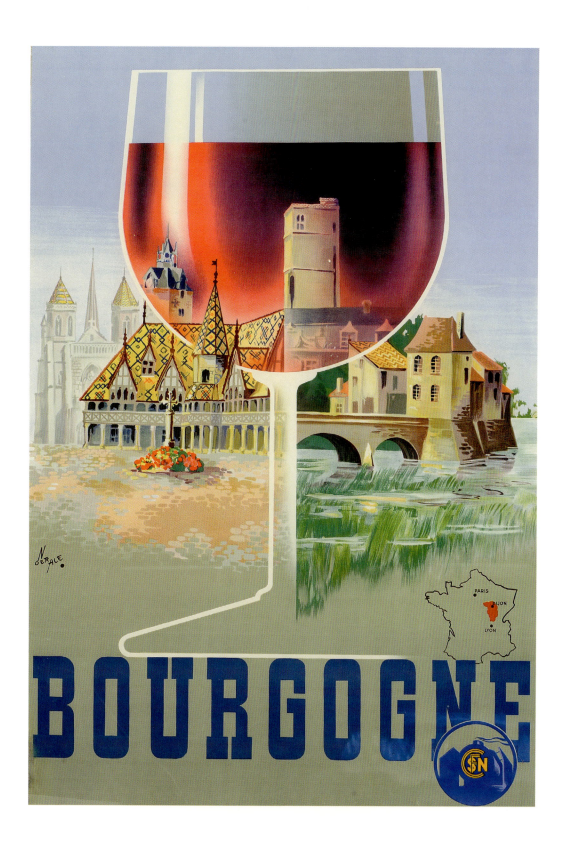

of commercialized celebration. But I know twenty Burgundians, starting with Aubert de Villaine, the owner of Clos de Romanée-Conti, or Jean Laplanche, the psychoanalyst-cum-winegrower of Pommard, whose bearing, manner, and conversation have more in common with a distinguished CEO—from Bordeaux, I almost wrote—than some sturdy redneck pulling on their suspenders before plucking a tasting cup wrapped in a rag from their pocket.

As for all French vineyards, responsibility for the estates and storehouses has been taken over by young men and women, some new to the business. They are ambitious on their own account—and thus, for their vines and their wines. Abandoning the unthinking facility of herbicides, they rely on the benefits of plowing. Convinced that only quality can guarantee their future, they limit production by reducing leafage and budding (*ébourgeonnage*) or by picking before the grapes are fully ripe (*vendange en vert*). Others have branched out into organic winegrowing. Or into biodynamics. For more than ten years now, Burgundy has been on the move, exploring, experimenting, emboldened to change whatever is outdated or redundant. Even the Hospices de Beaune are at it, entrusting their product to the English in wine auctions at Christie's in London.

If there is one real *vin de terroir*, rooted in its soil, in the bowels of its geology, it must surely be Burgundy. Here, every prestigious name is strictly delimited by the land registry, as well as by history and reputation. (Though, as Guy Renvoisé wrote in 1994, there have been the occasional compromises with heaven and with the quality controllers at INAO, in the case of Corton-Charlemagne, in particular.) The hierarchy of *grands* and *premiers crus* is enshrined by the lie of the land. And so is the hierarchy of the plots (dubbed *climats* here) within each *grands* and *premiers crus*. Historic Burgundy is a jigsaw puzzle, a pointillist tapestry. The villages have to share their fame with places, hamlets, and *climats* with pretty rustic names like Charmes, Rugiens, Blanches Fleurs, Clos des Chênes or Clos des Ormes, Ruchots, Petits Vougeots, Poulettes, Aux Combottes, Perrières, Au-Dessus des Malconsorts, Boucherottes, Bousse d'Or, Santenots Blancs, Santenots Dessous, Santenots du Milieu, Vergers, etc.

And there are hundreds of this ilk! One can either listen in wonder to the bucolic poetry that modern enology and trade have been keen to preserve; or else think ahead to the brutality of future business models that will doubtless result in the elimination

of these nuances of yesteryear. (For goodness sake, do away with *climats* when there are already no seasons to speak of!) In an increasingly standardized global market, it's certain that the soil of Burgundy—if winegrowers strive, year after year, to take only the best—will remain (as they used to say in bars on Wall Street) a blue-chip stock. The people of Bordeaux wax ironical about the parceling out of Burgundy vineyards, especially of Clos de Vougeot, which now numbers eighty owners and ninety plots over only fifty-one hectares. As Jean-Paul Kauffmann has said: "Nothing enduring can be built on such nit-picking." And yet owners or tenants of loft apartments are always astonished to learn one can survive happily in a studio flat. Or rather on two or three "barrels" (*pièces* of 228 liters [482 pints], in Burgundy). It's undeniable that concentrating the vines of Clos de Vougeot in fewer hands would render the appellation less ambiguous; and improve quality, too, since some of the smaller owners are tempted to overproduce so as to obtain a few more bottles. Still, it's been working fine like this for ages. And I envy those lucky enough to have inherited a few dozen acres of Clos de Vougeot, and feel sorry for the Bordeaux family that, finding it impossible to split up their château or meet death duties, is forced to sell up to a multinational.

Burgundy calls for tipplers endowed with singular force of character. It should not be downed when young and irresistibly sensual in its color, yellow with flashes of green, or vermilion or ruby; like a forbidden fruit, it makes one want to bite into it. With enological wisdom, we should be able to rein in our greed so as to down bottles condemned to a short life and lay down others destined to grow old with us. The former will vouchsafe us an explosion of flavor, from the garden in the case of the whites and from the orchard in the case of the reds; from the latecomers we will enjoy bouquets of subtle fragrance for which the palate and tongue have to be brought into play, as the nose alone is not up to the task.

If a young Burgundy possesses the immediacy of a confession, an old Burgundy harbors the attraction of an enigma. When I enjoy a young Burgundy, I ask it to excuse my impatience and raise my glass to the health of its elders. And when I sip an old Burgundy, I congratulate it on its patience and toast the memory of the young that are no longer with us.

Pages 60–61
Vendanges in ages past, as seen by Henri Cartier-Bresson, Burgundy, 1969.

Facing page
Grape-picking in the vines of Nuits-Saint-Georges, Côte de Nuits.

Charles Bukowski

It's September 22, 1978, on my TV literary show *Apostrophes*. As soon as I turn to my other guests, Bukowski grabs one of the bottles of Sancerre that had been placed at his request next to him and chugs it down. He then proceeds similarly to dispatch a second. Head thrown back, one cannot say he drinks it: he *downs* it, emptying the contents of each bottle directly into his body. It's a simultaneously fascinating and astounding spectacle. Unhindered, the wine seems to flow straight through his mouth and down his gullet: it is doing no more than obeying the law of gravity, as if sucked in directly by sheer vertical descent. His stomach rumbles and his chuntering drowns out the voices of the others. The humorist Cavanna quips: "Shut up, Bukowski!" When Bukowski advances a hand to grope authoress Catherine Paysan on the thigh, mortified she sits up, pulls down her skirt, and exclaims: "Oh, great! That takes the biscuit!" The audience roars with laughter. Bukowski carries on talking, drinking, burping, squirming about in his chair. Finally the Sancerre gets the better of him and he has to slouch off to the toilet. I don't chuck him off the set. But I don't call him back either. I remember saying at the time that, in the final analysis, Bukowski "doesn't seem able to hold his liquor."

In this I erred. The evidence conspires to show that, during this drunkard's life (and he didn't die prematurely, but at the respectable age of seventy-four), this undeniably talented storyteller and poet was, like Blondin, a world champion in alcohol consumption. Charles Bukowski was a curious sort of dipso: he marinated his despair in beer, but he needed the fuel of wine to write, guzzling it as he tapped on his typewriter keys.

His letters provide a lucid picture of the man: as if laughing, philosophizing, fabricating, confessing, writing, drinking, and having sex were all just ways of tricking himself out of a terror of life and death. His first publisher in France and an expert on his work, Gerard Guégan, wrote: "To a journalist who asked him whether 'drinking' wasn't a 'disease,' Buk replied that 'breathing' was a disease."

Facing page
Charles Bukowski wrote to his publisher that he got four superb poems out of a single bottle.

I only drink champagne when I'm happy and when I'm sad. Sometimes I drink it when I'm alone. When I have company I consider it obligatory. I trifle with it if I'm not in a hurry and drink it when I am. Otherwise I never touch the stuff, unless I'm thirsty.

Lily Bollinger

Down in the Cellar

To enter a cellar that a wine lover has lined with bottles is to descend into a world of silence, darkness, and serenity. Welcome, all, to the realm of the prone, the petrified. From miniature to jeroboam, all life is here: red and white, new and old, humble and glorious. Unlike our own, this world ages without fuss and bother, without laughter or complaint, in a rather damp placidity (dry-as-dust cellars—like dry-as-dust people—should be shunned like the plague), yet that doesn't mean there is not—between these four walls—energy, obstinacy, pride, joy, concentration, rumination, and philosophy.

The families gathered here together all bear names or appellations. All different, they have body and depth, color and tint, structure and texture, tannin and smoothness, sinew, nose, and finish, and even (as some call it) "legs." Wine may live its life behind glass, but it lives all the same. The great superiority of the cellar over the attic is that although both have a past, the cellar has a future too.

Though secured against snow and fog, Christmas and New Year's Day never take its denizens by surprise. Two or three degrees more, and it is summer; two or three less, winter. It cannot then be on such minute fluctuations in temperature that they base their experience of passing time. Born in step with the seasons, wine can still remember their variation. It knows too the vagaries of time, the swings of history. Firmly anchored in human chronology, at the end of each year, wine prepares to celebrate the arrival of the same Baby Jesus as in the previous winter, or the new vintage. It knows that it will flow copiously at both festivals. This is its task. This is its destiny.

It is not rare for a bottle to act as wallpaper for more than twenty, thirty years before, finally, taking front of stage at an exceptional soiree, in the glint of crystal, beneath the lights, gazed on by spectators, actors whose heads already swim at the mere mention of its name. A wine in the mouth is like a bull in the bullring: its apotheosis signals its death.

Even short-lived bottles, whose memory is likewise short-term— the Beaujolais, Bourgueils, Gaillacs, and Muscadets of this world— sense that the end of the year is not a time like any other. There

Page 66
Marilyn had a weakness for Piper-Heidsieck champagne. Here she's raising a glass on the set of *The Prince and the Showgirl*, with Laurence Olivier (1957), the only film she made in England.

Facing page
The historic cellar of Château-Lafite.

Facing page
A pyramid of light pours over the bottles in a cellar in Saint-Émilion, in the Bordeaux region.

are too many visits to the cellar, too much shuffling about. Usually unerring in his selection, the cellar owner hesitates. The only wine that is targeted immediately is champagne, armfuls of magnums regularly disappearing. Other bottles of wines are picked up cautiously, delicately, examined, put back. Moving from estate to château, from growth to *climat*, the longer he spends down there, the more perplexed he seems to be. His expression swings ceaselessly from interest to joy, from surprise to amazement. But then, he gives up. Turns out the light and shuts the door.

Only to return a few hours later. Or the next day. But this time he's done his homework. With a menu or recipe in mind for which, after due reflection, he has come up with a wine he hopes will fit perfectly—or at the very least prove intriguing. No sooner said than done, the elect glide off the rack. Already, he can sense, breathe them. The party begins to swing.

Like a safe, a cellar locks up a fortune in liquidity. But, unlike hard cash, it is liquidity that lives, breathes, ponders. Tomorrow sees the beginning of another year.

Cellars can be fussy—by which we mean, the closer your wine store approaches the ideal, the better its contents will keep. If your cellar is deep, north-facing, of near constant temperature in winter and summer (48°F–53°F/9°C–12°C), of steady humidity, neither exiguous nor enormous, protected from odor and vibration, and sheltered from daylight, your bottles will be glad of the chance to share some of their life in your domicile. But an imperfect cellar does not necessarily represent disaster: wines are tougher than is sometimes thought. In the long term, patently, they will succumb to the vicinity of a central heating radiator, to the emanations of a fuel-oil tank, to fermenting cheeses or rotting vegetables, to the after-tremors of the subway. But, apart from blatant assault and battery, wine has little against living conditions that demand vigor and character. There exists a kind of cellar fundamentalism that can make a man ashamed of possessing a *slightly* too arid vault directed southwest, or else be as puffed up as Dionysus to be making use of a dank, north-facing oubliette. Reveling in the latter residence, wine will not necessarily be imperiled in the former.

All the same, if you live in town, and can afford and have the space for it, dedicated air-conditioned wine storage offers an ideal means of preserving your bottles at a suitable temperature within easy reach of hand and mouth.

Left
A cellar is the setting for a key scene in Hitchcock's infernal 1946 thriller *Notorious*: two agents (Cary Grant and Ingrid Bergman) discover bottles of uranium concealed among the fine wines.

A meal without wine is like a day without sunshine.

Jean Anthelme Brillat-Savarin

Facing page In 1935, Cassandre, famous for some emblematic posters of the period, produced several designs for the wine merchant firm Nicolas, including this striking example (detail).

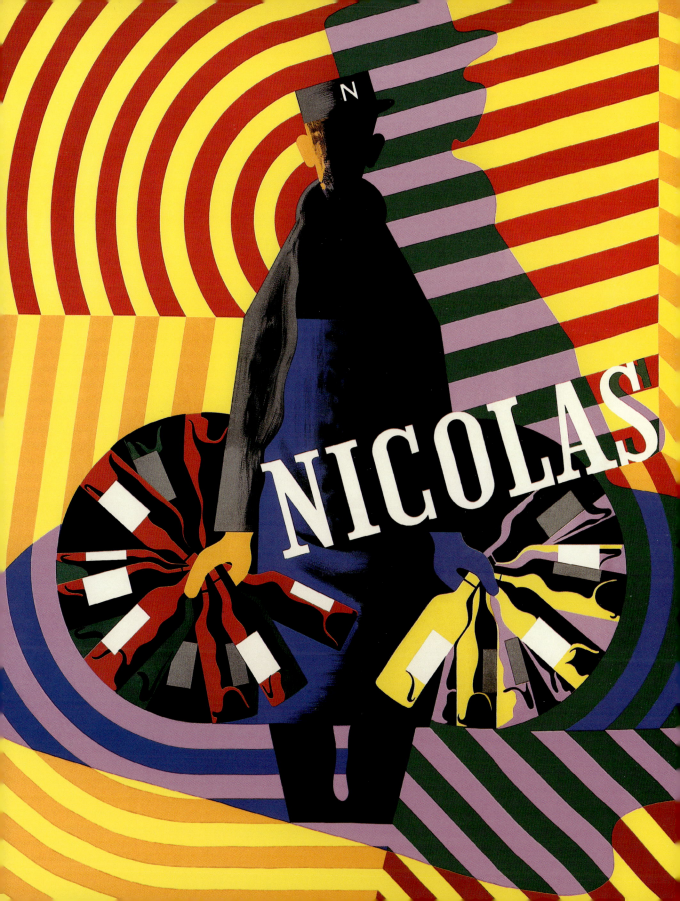

Champagne

To best appreciate the subtle flavor of champagne, one should have an empty stomach, or at the very least a fresh, spring-cleaned palate. This is why nowadays, abandoned at dessert, champagne has become desirable as an aperitif. Buoyant, relaxed, its feather-light bubbles invigorate nose and mouth alike. Lively and prickly, its gradual intromission sparks a particularly sharp pleasure, inciting and instigating other delights.

On the other hand, being treated to an old, even very old, champagne at dessert is all the more amazing because it has become such a rare occasion. In Rheims, Gérard Boyer was a dab hand at such happy endings. Bubbles three, four, five decades old with new-baked tidbits from the patisserie? "Oh my swallow-like lip!" Louis Aragon might have murmured. A truly venerable champagne adds to a simple and delicious apricot or peach tart notes of candied fruit that one won't forget in a hurry. In the course of a kind of earthly parody, the evening after her baptism, a glass of champagne is inverted over the head of Emma Bovary's daughter. Meanwhile, in Honoré de Balzac's *Lost Illusions*, Lucien de Rubempré's editor in chief "christens" him as a journalist by sprinkling a little champagne over his fair hair.

A magical wine, a most beneficial drink, and a good-luck charm, champagne is the natural accompaniment to life's turning points and other important events: it is hard to picture a wedding, a civil partnership, a birth, a promotion, an anniversary, a family reunion, or a retirement party without champers. Because it sparkles, because it foams, because it is merry, champagne is traditionally on hand at victories and successes, at triumphs or "firsts." Formula One drivers and motorcycle racers shake up huge bottles on the podium, while winning soccer and rugby players soak themselves in it in the locker room, in the process associating its image with a good hoedown rather than with classy dining. This phenomenon greatly enhances, it appears, the reputation of champagne, as it connotes youthful high spirits and sporting excellence. For a long time, a bottle or two was sacrificed on the hulls of newly launched ships. When a steamer crossed the Equator, the champagne flowed like water; in June 1950, the first men to climb to the summit of Annapurna, Maurice Herzog and

Facing page
"A meal served with nothing but champagne? Obviously, it's hardly an ordeal, but I'm too fond of a careful selection of white and red wines to deprive myself of their closer match with each dish." B. P.

Louis Lachenal, opened the single bottle of champagne laid down for them at camp No. 1. And was it Dieudonné Costes or Maurice Bellonte who said how he regretted not having taken a bottle with them on their non-stop flight across the Atlantic on September 1–2, 1930?

And yet, in the long-term, won't the overexposure of champagne—now for everyday consumption, as if it were just a wine like any other, to be served and guzzled just like any other, often at vast and deafening buffets—prove detrimental to its image of excellence and uniqueness?

Probably a victim of cultural prejudice, I don't like drinking champagne at any old time. All the more so since, at a do for five hundred people, the chances of being served Krug Grande Cuvée, a Salon, a Bollinger Tradition, a Cristal Roederer, a Deutz, a Pol Roger (cuvée Winston Churchill), a Ruinart rosé, a Demoiselle *millésimée* or a cuvée Grand Siècle by Laurent Perrier remain slim.

One can also be unexpectedly bowled over by bruts from little-known makers, but with two provisos: one has to be certain of their quality control and one has to allow the bottles to age in the cellar and so lose their early acidity. Thus the consumer has to do what, generally, due to lack of funds or space, the producer hasn't. I for one have always enjoyed Hervieux-Dumez's finest cuvées, bottles of which spend three or four years gravely meditating in my cellar.

There is an eternal question concerning champagne: is it invariably best to opt for vintage cuvées *millésimées* over traditional cuvées? The latter, the result of the blending of several years' harvest (sometimes as many as six or seven) and several varieties of vine (Chardonnay, Pinot Noir, Pinot Meunier), has the advantage of always offering virtually the same product—a house taste; even this evolves very slowly in the course of decades. The art of the head cellarman resides in judging a new harvest in accordance with the flavor of the earlier cuvées at his disposal, blending them so as always to obtain the unchanging product demanded by the customer. Such blending, or *assemblage*, entails uniformity, constancy, fidelity—it's like taking out a subscription.

On the other hand, vintage champagnes, cuvées *millésimées*, those produced only in great years, and more still when they are 100 percent Chardonnay, give rise to characteristic, original, one-off bottles. They bring something new. They introduce an element

Facing page
The vineyards of Champagne (here close to Rheims) extend over vast plains through scenery of monotonous charm.

of surprise. At bottom, they have more in common with a vintage wine than with classic champagne. And, since they are more expensive than admixed bottles of brut (even if it's only because they require aging longer in the 125 miles (200 km) of cellars and tunnels dug out of Champagne's chalky subsoil), consumers tend to be more radical in their appreciation. It is with a glass of vintage champagne in the hand that the most divergent, the most trenchant opinions are expressed. But it is here too that the most enjoyable encounters and the most rewarding discoveries take place.

Finally, for some time now, there has been a burgeoning market for *terroir* champagnes, vinified by named growers, which, on the Burgundian model, are the expression of a variety of vine, of a vintage, of a *cru*, of a man. These bottles are inevitably few and far between and their prices sky-high. Idiosyncratic and diverse, champagnes from little plots are not going to unseat the blended product of the great houses any time soon, but, around Épernay, they have been adding a touch of diversity, argument, and… effervescence.

Headline brands can boast both modernity and venerability. Ruinart is proud to declare itself "the oldest champagne house, since 1729," beating Moët et Chandon (1743) by a short head. But Gosset prints on its labels "*Aÿ-1584*" and in its advertising proclaims that it has "participated in all your celebrations, all over the world, since 1584." Seniority may be flaunted to show that the house has been doing what it knows best for a long time, that it is eternal, and that its consumers can enjoy total confidence. No one would dream of altering the shape of a bottle once it has etched itself into the collective consciousness. And, if this shape has become a classic, nothing will be changed in its decoration or label: they will never fall out of fashion, like the famous bottle with anemones that Emil Gallé created in the early 1900s for Perrier-Jouët.

Glugging champagne is unlikely to be conducive to serious financial or political discussion. It is a drink that encourages frivolity, a philosophy of laughter, trivialities. We choose themes whose nature can be compared to that of the wine: lightness, effervescence. Words are bubbles, the conversation sparkles. Exquisite moments. Champagne is not a wine for stick-in-the-muds.

Facing page
At the beginning of the nineteenth century, champagne houses began commissioning advertisements from artists such as Louis-Théophile Hingre. Théophile Roederer is today the second *marque* of the firm of Louis Roederer.

Pages 82–83
The Beatles having lunch, served with a jeroboam of Moët et Chandon, in a restaurant car at a London station during the shoot of *A Hard Day's Night* in 1964.

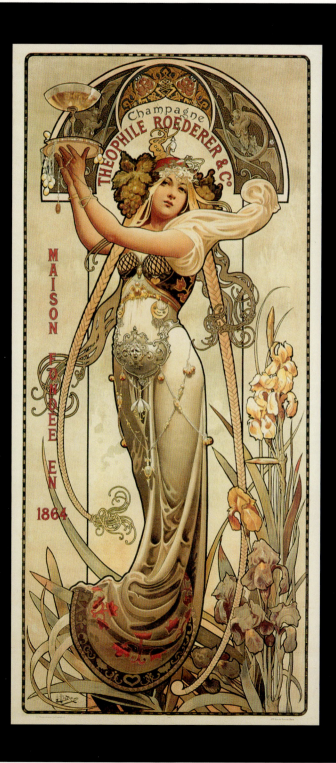

Chardonnay

Even vine varieties like a tease. Gamay, the type used for Beaujolais, is meant to have originated in Burgundy, at Saint-Aubin, in the hamlet of Gamay, while Chardonnay, which graces Burgundy white, is supposed to have first burgeoned in a village in the Mâconnais, duly called Chardonnay. Since the former emigrated to the south and the latter made its way north, they had to cross at Tournus, at Greuze, the restaurant created by the much-fêted French chef Jean Ducloux.

Like the round variety of football, the Chardonnay variety has conquered the world: it has put down roots in California, Spain, South Africa, Chile, and Australia. Easy to live with, companionable (and profitable), it has also taken up residence in Greece, Russia, Morocco, Canada, Japan, and China. In France, until the mid-twentieth century, it was employed exclusively in Champagne and Burgundy; it now sneaks in everywhere, even in the Languedoc, where it seems no longer put off by a pinch of frost. Nonetheless, Chardonnay, brave enough to plunge its roots into the chalk of Côte des Blancs, in Champagne, in the limestone of Chablis, and the stony soils of Montrachet, doesn't like getting cold feet. It's up there, in the polar regions, where the winter gets to you. But it is precisely the severity of the climate and its patient maturing process that confer its elegant, aromatic rigor.

Chablis. It is in the north of Burgundy that Chardonnay has to deal with the toughest winters. Replacing the traditional but only partially successful fires lit in *brûlots*, winegrowers (cut to the quick by the searing frosts of 1957 and 1961) decided to install among the vines of their *grands crus* and *premiers crus* a network of fuel-oil-burning "foot-warmers." Or else they sprinkle the stocks with water: by a curious paradox, a bud coated in ice better resists very low temperatures. Certain winegrowers stretch tarpaulins over their most valuable vines. Like Guy Roux, the iconic coach of the Auxerre soccer team for over forty years, the inhabitants of Chablis are an inventive, tough, wily people. But they have also yielded a little too much to the "French disease," and have overextended their vineyards. This has had no effect, of course, on the quality and reputation of wines produced where the

Facing page
A lithograph showing a bunch of Chardonnay grapes, from Pierre Viala and Victor Vermorel's *Ampélographie* (1910).

Benedictines long ago planted their vines: on the slopes around Chablis, on both banks of the River Serein. The floral, mineral tang of Chablis affords an impressive accompaniment to oysters. The same vintage goes just as well with fish or the cheese that follows.

Chassagne-Montrachet, Puligny-Montrachet, and Aloxe-Corton. These three villages produce, with Meursault, the best dry white wines in the world, no less. This is admitted even in the Bordeaux region! But, having been occupied for decades, this position is not necessarily guaranteed for all eternity. One has to face facts: France does not have a monopoly of the best soils nor of the finest vine technicians. This is why the Chardonnay of Côte de Beaune must avoid complacency and arrogance if it wants to keep ahead of competition from ambitious foreign upstarts.

The Montrachet (flanked by the marginally more modest Chevalier-Montrachet, Bâtard-Montrachet, etc.—no "the" needed, you note) is regarded as *the* best dry white wine in all Burgundy, and, consequently, on the planet. It's hard to check really: fewer than twenty acres (eight hectares) are harvested each year. Very chic, very expensive, very scarce: the *Mont-rare-chet!*

But it is not as if the other Montrachets—*premiers* and *grands crus*, all preceded by at least one name, such as Chevalier, Bâtard, Criots, Bienvenues (a heartfelt welcome to the most theatrical of them: Bienvenues-Bâtard-Montrachet!)—are going to be unearthed in the corner mini-market. Nor does Corton-Charlemagne hang about your local grocer's. Puligny-Montrachet and other "villages," less swanky and less pricey, are inevitably less rich, aromatic, and delicate than the aforementioned. Still, their more accessible pleasures are more than adequate.

And finally, on the Côte Chalonnaise, the Chardonnay grape finds delicate expression principally in the wines of Montagny, Mercurey, and Rully.

Mâconnais. If you prefer your Chardonnay to have a hint of hazelnut, toast, or honey, it is here that you can snaffle the best-value bargains. From the top of the rock of Solutré even François Mitterrand turned a presidential eye onto the vines of the seigneur of the region, Pouilly-Fuissé. Forty or so villages join their name with that of Mâcon. Saint-Vérand bequeathed its name to the pretty Saint-Véran (without the final "d" of the village, as if to subtly show that the same name is shared by other villages close to Saint-Vérand).

Facing page
This glass of South African Chardonnay demonstrates the extent to which this grape, originally from the region of Mâcon, has conquered the world.

Châteauneuf-du-Pape

It is self-evident that, in a Christian family, a bottle of Châteauneuf-du-Pape can be opened only on the Sabbath. Thus, in a space of a few hours, the scene shifts from a priest preaching temperance to a goblet of red "Pope" with the Sunday roast. This Holy Father is no slouch: concentrated, spicy, and peppery. Flavorsome when young, a venerable "Pope" has a bouquet of leather and tobacco. There was always someone who would pipe up: "It'd be even better with jugged hare!" It is my contention that the popes in Avignon used to hunt among the vines.

For centuries, Châteauneuf-du-Pape eked out a humble existence. Like its secular neighbors, Gigondas and Vacqueyras, it would take up the slack in years when Burgundy lacked alcohol or color. But, by the end of the nineteenth century, the winegrowers, forming a trade union, decided to toil for their own parish alone. The appellation has since been restored to the glory it enjoyed in the era of the Avignon papacy in the fourteenth century. In fact, the rules observed by winegrowers in the shadow of the Palais des Papes went on to inspire French national legislation on *appellations d'origines controlées* (AOCs: guarantees of origin and quality).

As believers trust in only one God, then logically a Châteauneuf should be single-varietal wine. And yet, it is one of the AOCs that contains the highest number of types of vine: thirteen! Eight for the reds; five for the white. Grenache is the cardinal of the reds, with, in its cortege, Syrah, Mourvèdre, and Cinsault. Counoise, Vaccarèse, Muscardin, and Terret Noir are mere acolytes. A similar office is held by Picpoul and Picardan for the white, where the floral incense of Roussane, Bourboulenc, and Clairette form a guard of honor for the consummate communion wine that is Châteauneuf-du-Pape.

Facing page
"So many numbers, but the year is the only really relevant one. At least twenty years of life for this prestigious Côtes-du-Rhône." B. P.

The Classification of 1855

One imagines that when members of the French National Constituent Assembly penned *The Declaration of the Rights of Man and of the Citizen* in 1789, they were convinced it would become a fundamental text and be destined to outlive them. Likewise, Napoleon's men of the law who drafted the Civil Code must have been confident of the importance and longevity of their enterprise. Nothing similar occurred to the wine-brokers of the Gironde, creators of a now celebrated document that has passed its one hundred and fiftieth birthday: the *Classement de 1855 des vins de Bordeaux* (known as The Classification). A routine task and one they had been ordered to perform, they would never have dreamed that it would continue to be referred to for decades and that even now its future seems guaranteed.

Curiously, Bordeaux winegrowers owe a scintilla of the success of their Classification to the rival groves of Champagne and Burgundy. Colleagues in these regions sent them a letter in which they proposed joining forces to present French wine at the Paris World Fair of 1855 that had been decreed by the newly enthroned emperor, Napoleon III. The owners of the Gironde had never entertained the notion. The offer was mulled over until some wily member of the Chamber of Commerce pointed out that it would hardly be judicious to let Champagne and Burgundy occupy the wine showcase in the exhibition all alone. Therefore, Bordeaux must attend; but they must send only produce of the highest quality.

Since since the end of the eighteenth century, wine merchants had been used to drawing up classifications of white and red wines in the Gironde, so the worthies of Bordeaux canvassed their opinion: on what basis would they establish their hierarchy? Why, on the market! The market was bound to be right, since it was founded on demand and this in turn depended primarily on quality. It was not the taste of the brokers themselves that decided: it was the enjoyment of the consumers. The Classification of 1855 is thus a rather early example of the liberal economy.

Acutely conscious of the significance of the task assigned them, and armed with generations of experience in drawing up prize lists, the brokers of the Gironde did not beat about the bush. Citing about sixty estates of reds based on market prices over a

Facing page
Sixty-one red *grand crus* appeared in the 1855 Classification, among them Boyd-Cantenac, the third *grand cru* from Margaux.

MOUTON

^{ON} DE ROTHSCHILD, Propriéta

1858

Galos

Gérant

BORDEAUX

Facing page
"First I am, second I was, Mouton does not change." This was the motto of Mouton Rothschild when in 1973 it joined the other four *premiers grands crus classés* in 1855.

period of forty years, they classified them, according to custom, into five categories. Thus they rewarded long-term quality and commercial success; but they had no doubt that it would be necessary to reexamine the order in subsequent years. The document was a classification for the World Fair of 1855, that was all. The assessment was intended to be temporary. Nobody could have imagined that it would amount to a birth certificate, a kind of creation myth. Moreover, if it had been seen at the time to be the Médoc equivalent of the Tablets of God's Law, it would have been stymied by an enraged coalition of excluded winegrowers. The Official Classification of 1855 (others came in its wake but none has gone down in history) thus owes its resilience and long life not only to its fairness, but also, more paradoxically, to its provisional nature, which thus ensured it was born without squabbling. Only Château Cantemerle was hastily added to the *cinquièmes crus* (fifth category), while, more than a hundred years later, Château Mouton Rothschild was elevated from the second to the first rank. Two codicils in a century and a half: not bad for a subject as imponderable as wine and something as constant as the owners' indefatigable desire for recognition.

Even if the path has been rocky on occasion, for one hundred and fifty years the sixty classified vintages have kept faith with their criteria, without which the entire Classification would have been sabotaged. Still, few of the vineyards possess the same borders as they did at the outset; the distribution of varietals has evolved; many owning families have changed or sold out to companies; the market has adjusted relative prices (certain fourth category wines, for example, are now worth as much as some seconds that may now equate to thirds; some *crus bourgeois* would also be worthy of elevation to the nobility). But no one's going to fiddle with the edifice now. The Classification is a listed monument! To seek to amend it would risk starting a war between châteaus of a ferocity that even the Middle Ages might have balked at. "Redrafting the Classification of 1855," notes Jean-Paul Kauffmann, an advocate of the status quo, "is an after-dinner pastime that has been going on for a hundred and fifty years. Sniping at that groundbreaking text is a favorite sport among wine journalists, sommeliers, and experts generally. But, instead of weakening it, controversy simply makes the organization even more solid, more stable, more alive. These sorties that benefit only the besieged end up by exasperating the besiegers!"

Blind tasting is to
wine drinking as
strip poker is to love.

Kermit Lynch

Blind Tasting

When the "sock" concealing the bottle's identity is withdrawn, tasters are often heard to let out an "oh!" of amazement or an "ah!" of disappointment. Stifled cries of pride tend to be in the minority. The old saying has it that blind tasting is a lesson in modesty. A humiliating ordeal, more like.

Let's put to one side, of course, the experts—sommeliers featuring in professional world championships whose memory for the innumerable wines they have tasted on countless occasions is simply flabbergasting. How on earth do they distinguish a Merlot from Chile from one from Greece, Australia, the United States, or South Africa? For one Alain Senderens, Jean-Claude Vrinat, or Jean Troisgros, who, year after year, would win the blind-tasting contest for Côte de Nuits at Mme Bise-Leroy's (joint owner of the Romanée-Conti property), how many other chefs, excellent at gauging tastes when the wine is known to them, are all at sea in the "masked ball" of the bottles? Some owners and winegrowers can't even recognize their own produce! The exceptionally gifted, the phenomenal, exist—on that we can agree. They have noses like radar and mouths as well equipped as an airliner cockpit. But the great majority of wine-lovers (even if they are just about able to explain what they feel, to analyze what they taste) operate in a Cloud of Unknowing when it comes to putting a name or a year to a Mystery Wine. Sometimes you get a bit lucky and are handed a bottle the like, or cousin, of which you've recently partaken, or land on a *terroir* that produces wines that have often tickled your tastebuds, or an appellation you can just about distinguish by comparing them with others you're pretty sure of. The worst is the unique wine, the solitary bottle that, without preparation, without notice, and thus without possible comparison, you are called upon to name. Always refuse this kind of balancing act, unless you have genius in your snout.

One evening, on my show *Apostrophes*, I played a mean trick on Émile Peynaud, the great Bordeaux enologist, who had just published a major book, *The Taste of Wine*. To spice up the program a bit, I asked my guests to guess the identity of a hidden wine. I really didn't want put Émile Peynaud through the mill or upstage him by choosing some rare, exotic, or left-field appellation. I had brought

Page 94
Bottle Rack (1914), the first ready-made, by Marcel Duchamp. This instrument is a familiar one to purchasers of wine in the barrel.

Facing page
Each year, Willi's Wine Bar in Paris commissions a poster on the theme of wine. This one, the first, was created in 1984 by Alberto Bali (detail).

up from my cellar a Haut-Brion 1970. I truly thought it would be child's play for him to recognize the world-famous *premier cru* from Graves. But I forgot the tension, close to panic, that grasps a man who suddenly becomes aware that he cannot, that he is not permitted to make a mistake, at the risk of losing all credibility. The pressure of being on live TV, all those eyes cruelly hoping the master would fall flat on his face, the heat of the spotlights, the uncomfortable set... Émile Peynaud tasted the wine, declared it poor, with a woody flavor, and decreed it a *petit cru*. The other guests, Christine de Rivoyre accompanied by her two sisters, were astonished and timidly advanced that it was delicious and that it might be, in their humble opinion, a Haut-Brion. Back in Bordeaux, it took some time for Émile Peynaud to recover from this mishap: it is said that he would drive miles out of his way to avoid the château of Haut-Brion. Selected precisely so he might shine with little effort, my initiative, in forgetting the untoward effects of stage fright, had resulted in mortification. Albeit of a rather different nature, my own was no less painful.

Blind tasting is useful when it is collective and its purpose is to ensure that a label can be affixed to a wine in conformity with its appellation; that is, either to grant a stamp of quality to wines which, with the same appellation, were considered superior to others, or to award medals, cups, trophies, diplomas, and so on to various products at competitions. Blind tasting might also help inform and guide consumers in their purchases, with selections that might be wide-ranging and sizable (*Hachette Guide to French Wines 2005* announces 32,000 wines tasted and 10,000 chosen), regular and critical (thus with the weekly magazine supplements devoted to wine after the vacation every September, ever since *Le Point* and Jacques Dupont launched the fashion in 1999), or for a target audience (for example, the "buyer's guide" issued with each number of *Bourgogne Aujourd'hui* (Burgundy Today), the jury comprising merchants, enologists, winegrowers, sommeliers, specialized journalists, etc., as well as non-professionals). When they take place around a few tables, blind tastings can be amusing, especially if, after each wine, the game is to comment and grade it on an austere report card. Among four, five, or six testers—as among hippopotamuses and turkeys—there is always one dominant. Not inevitably a male. They will be a professional or a drinker rubicund with experience, whose every gesture will be scrutinized by their table companions. Carefully noting his or

Facing page
An improvised "blind" tasting of Dom Pérignon. "Drinking champagne, one feels an urge for frivolity, for a sunny outlook, for silliness."
B. P.

her onomatopoeias, the others concur with remarks let slip all the more readily as the expert is aware of the influence they might have. A sniff, a smack of the lips, several spits; if he or she is unsure the whole table hesitates too and bobs its nose again. For this is a good sign for the wine. If a single, cursory examination satisfies, though, followed at once by a judgment scribbled without a second thought, the whole table frowns: an execution is on the cards.

But does one back up one's opinions? Enological vocabulary is of such richness that only fluent speakers are able, at speed, orally or with pen in hand, to find just the right words and expressions to describe their impressions. As in other domains of culture, science, and technology, there are initiates, gurus, and high priests, and then poor, earnest toilers who spend their whole life getting to grips with the transcendental jargon. I am of the latter stripe, even if I can hold my own for a few appellations, I've been imbibing since infancy—but always with the prudence of someone who never forgets that even the most familiar wine can fall out of line or turn traitor. Then there are others that look as if they're from some distant land but turn out to be a close neighbor sporting a plastic nose.

It has always seemed to me that a wine's *length* (experts measure this in *caudalies*) is a touch more flattering when it is drunk instead of spat out. As if it wanted to reward the taster for rescuing it from the unworthy fate of expulsion. When it's good, I forget, I confess, the presence of the infamous bucket. As someone—I can't recall who—once said: "When it's good, I spit it *inward*."

"The story of two coopers-cum-gourmets called to deliver their opinion on an owner's wine is well known. The first tasted it and pronounced: 'The wine is good, but tastes of leather.' The second tasted in his turn and declared: 'I do not share my colleague's opinion. This wine is good, but it tastes of iron.' Voicing his astonishment the owner swore that his wine had never been in contact with either leather or iron. The day the cask was emptied, however, there was found, right at the bottom, a tiny key tied to a strip of leather that had fallen into it by accident. And thus was the subtle knowledge of the two tasters demonstrated to all." André Theuriet, quoted in René Mazenot, *Le Tastevin à travers les âges* (Wine Tasting Through the Ages).

Facing page
"Pleasure of the nose" is one of eight illustrations created by Charles Martin, often to be seen on the walls of superior wine bars.

Wine is bottled poetry.

Robert Louis Stevenson

Facing page "A poster ought to afford the solution to three problems: optical, graphic, and poetic," wrote Cassandre, who created this poster for Nicolas wines in 1935.

God and Wine

The Promised Land. Though wine runs in torrents through the Bible from Genesis to the Gospels (and particularly in Solomon's Song of Songs), I am not one of those who would like a note in each copy to advise reading "only in moderation." Sometimes guilty of making men drunk, sometimes a promise of wisdom, wealth, and happiness, wine is inextricably bound up with the human condition. It can lead men astray or guide them back to the straight and narrow. God placed wine at the disposal of men so that, left to their own devices, they might use it for better or for worse.

God gave Noah the vine. God did not present Noah with hops, rice, sisal, or any other plant from which the six-hundred-year-old might have fermented alcohol. The vine was a divine gift. Thus, the Creator enshrined the preeminence of wine over all other alcoholic beverages. He permitted the vine and wine to find their place in Holy Writ (they are mentioned no less than 441 times) and in the sacred chapter of human memory. This is one of the reasons that I find dietitians treating wine so cavalierly, as if it were just one alcoholic drink among others, so unacceptable.

Since Noah discovered wine, it was only to be expected that he would become its first victim. There were to be others. Intoxication is shameful, whereas a rightful and natural love of wine brings strength and merriment. Drunkenness is condemned, especially in kings. The "writers" of *Prophets* admit that wine may give succor to "those with bitterness in their soul." The Old Testament is effectively the first moral treatise on wine.

The most spectacular viticultural image is probably that comparing the Promised Land with a vine that will one day give forth fruit and wine to the Chosen People. It is the Hebrews' hope that they might transplant vinestocks from Egypt to the land of Israel. This is precisely what Nicolas Poussin shows in his 1660–64 picture *Autumn* (a.k.a. *The Bunch of Grapes Taken from the Promised Land*; The Louvre). Two men are crossing a valley (see left), with the ends of a pole resting on their shoulder: from the middle hangs a gigantic bunch of red grapes, a symbol of the promise of freedom, prosperity, and peace.

"*For this is my blood.*" It is thanks to the Gospels that wine has become the mystical drink par excellence. Not that the assimilation of blood and the juice of the vine presents much of an innovation. The comparison is plain as a pikestaff. It did not escape Osiris that this was a way of impressing his worshippers. But Jesus plainly identifies himself with the vine:

I am the true vine, and my Father is the gardener.... I am the vine; you are the branches.... If you do not remain in me, you are like a branch that is thrown away and withers; such branches are picked up, thrown into the fire, and burned.
(John, 15: 1, 5–6)

Out of twenty-four parables in the Gospels, four concern vines and wine—not counting the famous miracle of the Wedding at Cana. Throughout his public life, Jesus refers to wine and drinks it. It is not sacrilege then for certain châteaus in Bordeaux to bear the name Évangile or Angélus, or for a wine from the Campania to be known as Lacryma-Christi (Tears of Christ).

Before he was put to death, at the final meal he took with his Apostles, Jesus made bread and wine the most important and popular food and drink in the Western world. Two millennia later, this is still the case. In fact, with the exception of Jesus himself, the bread and the wine were the two most significant guests at the Last Supper. And very quickly, these three became one.

According to Matthew and Mark, the bread was consecrated before the wine; according to Luke, it was the other way round. (John says nothing on the subject. Had Luke acquired the habit of kicking off meals with a glass or two?) The episode is best recounted in Matthew:

And as they were eating, Jesus took bread, and blessed it, and brake it, and gave it to the disciples, and said, Take, eat; this is my body. And he took the cup, and gave thanks, and gave it to them, saying, Drink ye all of it; For this is my blood of the new testament, which is shed for many for the remission of sins. But I say unto you, I will not drink henceforth of this fruit of the vine, until that day when I drink it new with you in my Father's kingdom. (Matthew 26:26–29)

The last sentence requires explanation from a Gospel exegete or Vatican cellarman. Jesus announces that he will not drink again until the day his Disciples join him in the kingdom of heaven. They've been together some two thousand years. But we hardly picture them leaning against a sideboard, feasting and quaffing as if at a school reunion. That's not their style. Nor does it seem to imply that, after the Last Judgment, God intends to offer drinks all round to Jesus and the elect.

Pages 104–5
Autumn, or *The Bunch of Grapes Taken from the Promised Land*, Nicolas Poussin, 1660–64.

Facing page
Melchizedek, the first priest in Christian history to perform the offering of bread and wine. French School, seventeenth century.

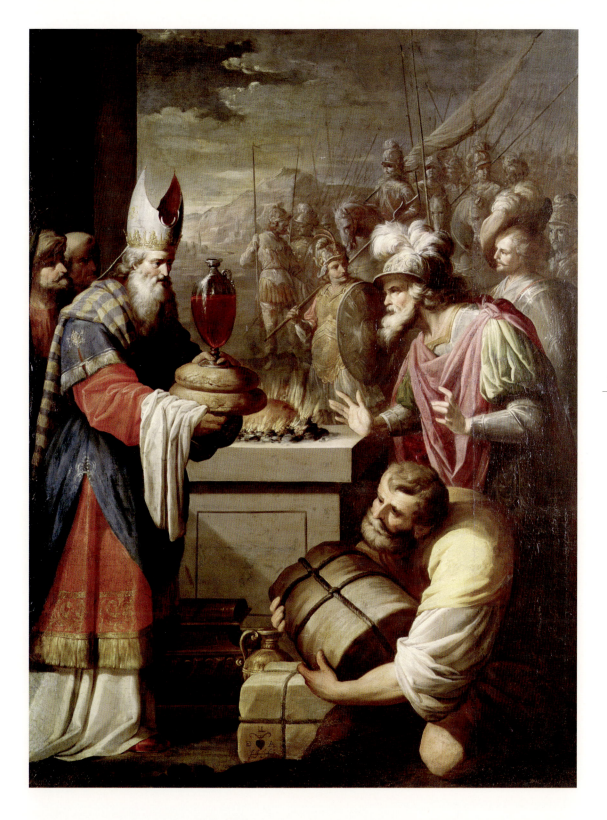

Dom Pérignon

For inventing the champagne method and thus bringing into our valley of sorrows such exquisite pleasure, Dom Pérignon should have been canonized long ago. Dom Pérignon added to the sum of happiness in the world, and, for that, he deserves to be if not a saint, then at least one of the blessed.

If the Church did ever decide to honor those ecclesiastics who have made champagne such a gift from God, in addition to the Benedictines of the Abbey of Hautvillers, whose cellarman Dom Pérignon was, and where Dom Ruinart earned his renown, the monks of Saint-Basle and Saint-Thierry would be good candidates. But then there were many monks who were winegrowers, cellar masters, and wine merchants, so closely is the history of the Champagne region and wine bound up with that of Christendom.

Whether Dom Pérignon was truly the inventor of bubbles is a subject of debate. His supporters base their preference on a passage in a letter (1821) from Dom Grossard, *procureur* (chief steward) of the Abbey at Hautvillers: "It is Dom Pérignon who discovered the secret of making sparkling white wine, because, before him, there was only *vin paillé* and *vin gris*." His detractors, however, have produced documents, according to which champagne sparkled before Dom Pérignon's first vintage.

Still, the majority of historians agree that it was the Dom who first came up with the revolutionary idea of mixing growths, thus offering champagne such a vast range of subtle tastes. If it was probably not Dom Pérignon who introduced the cork stopper, he did invent several processes that increase the quality of sparkling wine, in particular the operations of *collage* (adding finings), as well as bottle closing. That's more than enough to earn him endless gratitude and eternal life.

Regarded as one of the great champagne vintages, as well as one of the best, and marketed in a bottle whose admirable shape makes it instantly recognizable and popular, adorned for decades with a classic label, Dom Pérignon often makes an appearance in detective and spy novels, as well as in regular fiction. It is always associated (though this might perhaps be said of any champagne) with the celebration of some extraordinary event.

Facing page
Bas-relief representing Dom Pérignon in St. Peter's Abbey at Hautvillers, to the north of Épernay. This abbey is today the property of the House of Moët et Chandon; it holds receptions there.

That nectarous, delicious, precious, heavenly, joyful, and divine liquor called wine.

François Rabelais, *Pantagruel*

Label Art

There is an etiquette, a ceremony, observed whenever wine is presented and served at a royal, aristocratic, or simply swanky junket. Wine pourers—*échansons* (such a pretty word in French)—possessed the rank of officer of the household. They had learned the art of pouring their masters' nectar into the guests' glasses. They did not do this at table, but on a sideboard, a dresser in the feast hall, most frequently at the beginning and end of the meal. Wine waiters are the cupbearers of democracy. Today they are less sticklers for etiquette and more worried about the wine labels, and the strips round the neck and the wordier panels on the other side of the bottle—packed with interesting information on the wine and the estate or else awash with commercial lather singing the praises of some filthy hooch. Just like an ID card, or an obligatory business card, on which makers are mandated to provide information on the product, its appellation, and alcohol content, as well as the name and address of those responsible for it, and so on. On a full bottle, a label is as promising as a visa; on a pathetic, empty bottle, it is more like an inscription on a tombstone.

The label also testifies to the artistic taste, or otherwise, of the owner or merchant. It is on the label fixed to the glass that man and wine are most closely linked, inextricable from purchase until the last drop has been ingested. I learned how to enjoy Bordeaux through its labels. At that time, the lettering on Burgundies and Beaujolais was very often a portentous, pretentious Gothic. A Bordeaux, by comparison, reeked of understated elegance. The label sits better on a Bordeaux than on a Burgundy, not only due to the elongated shape of the bottle (tubbier for the latter), but also because a majority of lords of the manor in the Gironde have, since time immemorial, lavished more attention on its aesthetics (and therefore to attracting potential customers) than that normally vouchsafed by growers on the Côte-d'Or. In Bordeaux, there was also the need to appeal to the English on the bottle. As the Bordelais Pierre Veilletet says: "For a wine, the label represents the written exam sat before taking the oral." Can a wine hide mediocrity behind a splendid label? Yes, just as we all know that a scheming mind can be draped in a thousand-dollar suit. Still, such impostures, it seems to me, are more rare among

Page 110
A glass of Yquem. The elegant graphic simplicity of this wine's label is exemplary.

Facing page
Since 1945, every year Mouton Rothschild calls upon the talents of an artist of international renown to illustrate its labels. The label on this 2005 vintage, one of the estate's finest, is by the sculptor Giuseppe Penone.

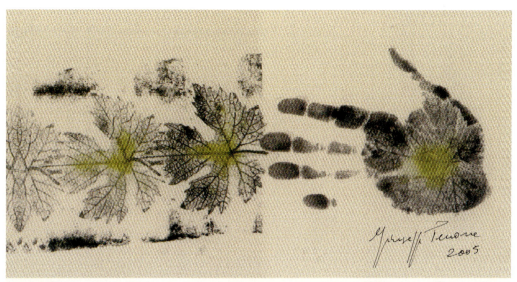

Dessin inédit de   *Giuseppe Penone*

2005

toute la récolte a été mise
en bouteilles au Château

Philippine de Rothschild

Château
Mouton Rothschild®

PAUILLAC

13 % Vol.   APPELLATION PAUILLAC CONTROLÉE   75 cl

Baronne Philippine de Rothschild g. f. a.

PRODUCE OF FRANCE   PROPRIETAIRE

bottles than among humans. In fact, correlation between the style of a wine and that of its label tends to be the rule. The brash vulgarity of artwork on so-called "table" wines is as apparent as the class of those on the finest growths. The graphic designer and art director (terms that did not exist in those remote ages, when the labels on the great champagnes or the prestigious vintages of Bordeaux and Burgundy were conceived) seem to have been inspired—for good or ill—by what they had been drinking. The elegant, graphic simplicity of the label on a Château d'Yquem cannot be bettered (all the more so since, in 1975, the Lur Saluces family was authorized to relegate the obligatory legal buff onto a strip stuck *underneath* the label). Every year since 1945, Mouton Rothschild has commissioned their label from a famous artist. This has enabled masterpieces to see the light of day. The label most sought after by collectors, the 1924 version by the poster designer Jean Carlu, is clever but too full. In their sobriety of line and artwork, some of his predecessors were admirable. My friend, the writer Maurice Chapelan, has it that great writers and great artists "proceed from distortion to rectitude and from ornament to sparseness." Bordeaux labels have not all followed this rule, judging by some old and splendid labels on Châteaus Léoville, Pichon-Longueville, Lafite, Brane-Cantenac, Palmer, Léoville-Poyferré, on the Philippe Parès collection; these were affixed by wine merchants, it is true, and long preceded the stringent legislation on the information that has to appear on them now.

The labels currently on Haut-Brion, Ausone, Lafite-Rothschild, and Margaux are not bad, but no better than that. The Pétrus label is rather clichéd (what I have just written will sound to some as gross and unforgivable as if I'd claimed that *King Lear* was not up to much). But all are historic monuments. Like the frontage of a listed building, they should be left unaltered. Even if producers in other French vineyards have, over the last thirty years, considerably improved the design of their labels (some, in the wake of the generally more inventive Italians, shaking up the traditional approach completely), the best in this field remain those of the Bordeaux and Champagne regions.

Facing page
"Georges Duboeuf's bold and sure taste has allowed him to revolutionize the idea of the wine label with the fragrant gaiety of his flowers: violet for Chiroubles, field poppy for Beaujolais, honeysuckle for Pouilly-Fuissé, etc." B. P.

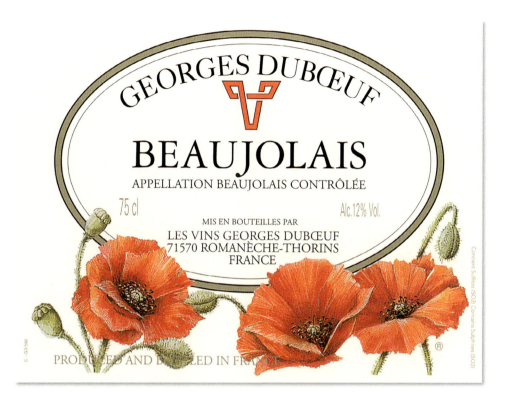

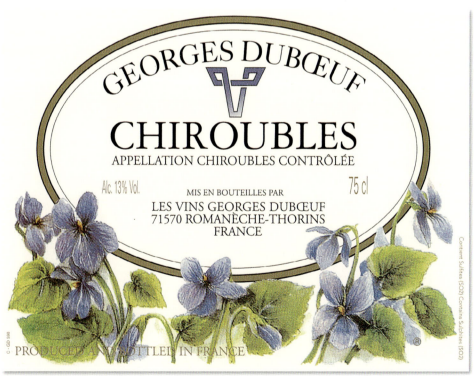

> Not the least pleasure of wine is [its] Madeleine-like ability to reawaken previous pleasures, to transport us back in time and place.
>
> Jay McInerney, *A Hedonist in the Cellar*

Haut-Brion

In the Classification of 1855, dealing with the red wines of Bordeaux, there is an eccentricity, an incongruity, almost: to the sixty vintages of the Médoc, a sixty-first is added, which is not from the same parish. In fact it hails from Pessac, on the outskirts of Bordeaux, and it is a Graves: Haut-Brion. And it was not included through gritted teeth, buried somewhere in the list. On the contrary, it is enshrined as the equal of the top three vintages of the Médoc: Lafite, Latour, and Margaux (Mouton joined much later).

It was not through the goodness of their soul that Médoc growers granted a place in the sun to this rival from the south, but because the quality and prestige of Haut-Brion were already such that it would have been inconceivable to exclude it from the list. Those who would never have countenanced such ostracism were Bordeaux's best customers: the English. In London, the "Ho, Brian," as it was known, enjoyed an unequaled reputation, notably because of a very chic, long-lived tavern that opened after the fire of London (1666), where the French owner of Haut-Brion served his wine exclusively. In this place one might, apparently, run into authors Daniel Defoe or Jonathan Swift. The sign over the haunt read "Pontac" (Pontack's House), in tribute to Jean de Pontac, a contemporary of statesman and author Michel de Montaigne (1533–92). De Pontac was a real bright spark who, at Haut-Brion (which was acquired partly by marriage, partly through purchase), concocted the concept of the "wine château." The vines grew on a soil that suited them, while the château was built on less promising land—a model for all his successors in the region. If the Graves is regarded as the ancestral haunt of the great wines of Bordeaux, they owe it to Jean de Pontac and his lineage at Haut-Brion. Certain historians record a classification dating to 1640 in which the Graves wines precede the Médoc. The latter has since wreaked its revenge, though it has the grace to welcome at its table the prestigious suburban commuter from Bordeaux.

Page 116
In the cellars of the Canarelli domain, on the south coast of Corsica.

Facing page
An Haut-Brion 1961 quietly aging in the château's cellar. The bottles are gradually covered in the mold characteristic of a great cellar.

I feel sorry for people who don't drink. When they wake up in the morning, that's as good as they're going to feel all day.

Frank Sinatra

Persian Bards

Of venerable enological tradition, Persia was the land in the Muslim world where the love of wine was the strongest—or the least hidden. It is also from Persia that the best poets of wine came.

There was that odd chap, Abû Nuwâs: a libertine and bacchic poet, who wrote in Arabic and preferred boozing in taverns and nights in the bordello to pilgrimages to Mecca. Born al-Hasan ibn Hani Al-Hakami, Abû Nuwâs (meaning "with the curly hair") lived, loved, and drank from 756–814 CE. In almost all his verse, Abû Nuwâs celebrates wine, "the wine of Babylon," "the wine of Karkh" (a district in Baghdad). He knows that the Prophet prohibited its consumption, but he imbibes anyway and takes his punishment of eighty strokes of the lash. He drinks wine because it gives him pleasure, assuages his sorrows, makes him tipsy or just plain drunk: "Once tasted, we sail through the ether, / Jettisoning reason and propriety alike."

Abû Nuwâs cannot imagine a love affair or a sex act, whether with a woman or a beautiful youth, without it being accompanied by wine. Wine for him is synonymous with freedom.

In the West, the best known of these rollicking, insolent poets is without question the author of the *Rubáiyát* ("quatrains"): Omar Khayyám, a native of Naishapur, Persia (now Iran), who was born in 1048 CE. Poet, but still more mathematician, algebraist, astronomer, this illustrious scholar blithely flouted the Qur'an and religious authority with the wine of Shiraz (his favorite), and sung of its delights and virtues. Like his predecessor, Abû Nuwâs, he opted to make a name for himself as a hedonist on this earth rather than put all his hopes in the joys of the next world: "Ah, take the cash and let the credit go."

Persia's literary tradition is entwined with the vine. As fourteenth-century poet Shamsudin Muhammad Hafiz (Hafez) wrote: "A rose without the glow of a lover bears no joy; / Without wine to drink, the spring brings no joy."

Page 120
Drinking a bumper of red at the counter of a bar in Paris in 1955.

Facing page
A portrait of a youth signed by "the humble painter Ahmad." The elegance of the figure is in keeping with the delicate crystal glass and carafe containing the wine of which Persians were notoriously fond.

Wine... can spark strong emotions
or draw a tear for the ethereal beauty of the thing.

Richard Olney, *Lulu's Provençal Table*

Facing page As if with an artist's brush, wine paints the surface of the wooden barrels.

Drunkenness

I am not an advocate, nor even a defender, of intoxication. Too many crimes, too many accidents, too many horrors in word and act, too much rudeness and madness, too much raving, too much numbness, too much staring into space—as if someone else, someone violent, slobbering, staggering, idiotic had slipped into one's abandoned, vacant body. "The worst state of man," Michel de Montaigne wrote in the sixteenth century, "is when he loses the awareness and the governance of himself."

Diderot (no teetotaler) stated: "Intoxication puts out every glimmer of reason, totally extinguishing that particle, that spark of divinity that differentiates us from brute beasts; it thus destroys all the satisfaction and consideration each of us ought to give and receive from human intercourse."

Vocabulary. Drunkard, drunk, sot, boozer, alkie, soak, dipso, dip, whisky-nose, swillpot, sponge, stewbum, rummy, tippler, inebriate, boozehound, sozzler, tank, juicehead, tosspot, soak, newt, soaker, red-nose, lush, imbiber, souse, barfly, rumpot, guzzler, wino, bottle-man, bibbler, toper, binger, pub-crawler—a caskful of words to designate the inveterate drinker!

Literature. "Nathanael, let me speak to you of drunkenness," André Gide tell us in *The Fruits of the Earth*. Through Ménalque, the imaginary master, the author acknowledges: "I have known the drunkenness that makes one think one is greater, grander, richer, more virtuous, more respectable, etc. than one really is."

Baudelaire: "I've known an individual whose enfeebled sight regained all its piercing power when drunk. Wine changed the mole into an eagle" (*Artificial Paradises*). And Baudelaire again, the greatest poet of wine, supreme in his daydreams, his backsliding and startling insights: "One ought to be drunk at all times. That's it: *that* is the only question. Not to feel the dread burden of Time that bends down your shoulders and pushes you to the ground, you have to be drunk without stint. But with what? With wine, poetry, or virtue, as you like. But get drunk" (*Paris Spleen*).

Though it will be observed that it is easier to get drunk with wine than with poetry, and more still than with virtue. Verlaine confessed: "Ah! if I drink, it's to get drunk, and not for the drink" (*Jadis et naguère*). Apollinaire ends his alcoholic collection, *Alcools* (Alcohols, 1913), with a long poem entitled "Vendémiaire" (after the name of the first month of the French republican calendar), in which he exalts an unquenchable thirst, initially, of French, then European, and finally universal scope:

I am drunk with drinking the whole universe
On the quayside from where I watched the waters racing and the bilanders slumber
Listen: I'm the gullet of Paris
And if I like I'll go on to drink the universe
Harken to my songs of universal drunkenness.

There is a difference, however, between authors who depict wholesale or historic benders in their works (as in Rabelais, Balzac, Alexandre Dumas, Zola), and those innumerable writers, French and foreign ("Shut up, Bukowski!"), who are simply card-carrying alcohol fiends, incorrigible soaks, paid-up members of the Katzenjammer club. These can be described in the same manner as drinkers who don't write: such authors hit the bottle because they are desperate or over-confident, poor or rich, slavish or domineering, weak-willed or cynical, unhinged or blasé. Or simply because they enjoy wine, beer, whisky, vodka, or whatever. Because they look forward to the intoxication it gives and which their body and mind craves. Still, above and beyond their hackneyed excuses, there is perhaps a mysterious bond between writing and alcohol, characteristic of the trade. Social philosopher Guy Debord says: "Writing will surely remain rare, since before excelling in it one has to have drunk for a long time." As if writing flowed from alcohol and texts from the bottle. Or as if, for certain writers, an unlubricated quill, one trimmed with temperance, can only align words without savor, without sap, flat and—yes—watery.

Writing is a journey; so is drunkenness. Neither is without dangers. Both conduct the intrepid to countries without frontiers, up mountains to be found on no map, down into uncharted valleys, back to bygone ages or forward to times yet to come; both meet acquaintances they don't recognize, as well as unknown people they know all too well.

Literature and drunkenness are both *vanishing lines. Passwords.* Days of tasting and bushels of dreams. Have you ever

Pages 126–27
Gazing vaguely out, *The Young Taster* (1740), painted by Philippe Mercier, contemplates the glass without really seeing it. He is not intoxicated: just a bit tipsy.

Facing page
The man's hand and the wine cup stand out against the girl's yellow tunic. Both have had a drink and she is ready to yield. Vermeer was twenty-four when he painted *The Procuress* in 1656.

Pages 130–31
"If I drank less, I'd be a different man, and that's not for me." Jean Gabin in Henri Verneuil's movie based on a novel by Antoine Blondin, *A Monkey in Winter* (1962), costarring Jean-Paul Belmondo.

noticed how a writer, even if he's signed the pledge, and someone who's had a skinful often seem to be *elsewhere*? And, if one believes Persian and Arabic poets of inebriation, there even exists a metaphysics of intoxication.

Just one more glass, wine waiter, and I will finally decipher the glorious and eternal enigma that the pens of all writers worthy of the name have pursued: the Enigma of Time. It is always at the bottom of the last goblet that God is to be found. I've never actually looked there, probably because I'm not a writer. Thus have I never yielded to true inebriation.

Wasted, but nice. If many soaks are cantankerous, sinister, or plain nasty, others seem tenderized by booze. Topers who, out on the binge, retain a sunny and devil-may-care philosophy of existence. Splicing the mainbrace plunges them into a sort of euphoria they desperately want to communicate to their drinking companions, and even to innocent bystanders. They belt out songs about being drunk or head over heels in love. The voice is often gravelly, but that doesn't worry them. They may even be interesting. I knew someone back in Lyon: tall, waif-like, wan, clad in austere black and with a tie, who riffed on Plato, Theocritus, Pascal, and Anatole France in front of corpses of Morgon or Chiroubles, before suddenly keeling over plum in the middle of a recitation of Paul Valéry's esoteric 1917 work *La Jeune Parque* (The Young Parca). One looks on these fragile barflies with a kindly eye—what is the mysterious reason behind their dipsomaniacal distress? There is elegance in their disorder, and panache and verve in their pathetic bravura. In this vein are the unforgettable friends Quentin and Fouquet during their ethylic and tauromachian frenzy on the Normandy coast (in Antoine Blondin's *A Monkey in Winter*). Or again, Nick Molise in California (in *The Brotherhood of the Grape* by John Fante), a hooch-hound exercising his elbow in a dilapidated Italian café and sowing trouble and strife among his family. Starting out awful yet likeable, he dies having earned our compassion and sympathy.

> We thought of wine as... a great giver of happiness and well-being and delight.... It was as natural as eating and to me as necessary.
>
> Ernest Hemingway

Krug

Like "Citroënists" (they only drive Citroën cars), "Krugists" consider no champagne other than Krug worthy of their table and tastebuds. Away from home, they don't go so far as to refuse to partake of a bottle of Pol Roger, Ruinart, or Roederer. (In the same way, a "Citroënist" may deign to accept a lift in a Renault or an Opel if it fits in with their plans.) But they are committed to Krug with the same enthusiasm, the same intolerance as others are to Mustangs or Ferraris.

According to Father Bernard Bro, Julien Green never served him a champagne other than Krug. The Franco-American author was thus a fully paid-up "Krugist", like Hemingway and Paul Morand, to confine myself to authors who now only drink on Olympus. Since their day, even if Krug (with Salon) is the most expensive of all champagnes, its circle of admirers, famous and unknown, has widened considerably, even reaching Japan.

From the forefather Joseph Krug (1800–1866) to Henri, the winegrower, cellar master, and craftsman, with Remi, his brother, merchant, and ambassador, Krug has always been a bit of a lone wolf, reckoning that the exceptional quality of their champagne and its limited production deserve respect and demand a price with which the majority of experts agree. Masters of the craft? They lay claim to its method and spirit. Artists? They don't go that far. Henri has, however, published a small tome entitled *L'Art d'être Krug* (The Art of Being Krug), in which he compares the Grande Cuvée to a symphony and the Clos du Mesnil (a tiny and admirable single varietal) to a sonata. To hail forty years of blending, racking, and creativity, Rémi threw a sumptuous dinner (Krug 1988, Krug rosé, Krug Collection 1979) at the Cité de la Musique for his brother Henri and the great and good of cultural Paris. Suffice it to say that the two brothers' profiling and marketing strategy is entirely oriented toward creation, the arts, and cultural exclusiveness, a decision that has earned them jealousy and the occasional stab in the back. They couldn't care less. Business-wise, the "Krug cult," founded on the quality in their atypical bottles, is in sparkling form.

Page 132
Black and White Café (1972–73), by Patrick Caulfield, an English pop artist who frequently depicted bars, cafes, and other interiors.

Facing page
At Krug, the grape harvest is done by hand, as it was in 1843.

Page 136
An old-fashioned Burgundy bottle of Romanée-Conti.

The simple act of
opening a bottle
of wine has brought
more happiness to
the human race than
all the collective
governments in
the history of earth.

Jim Harrison

Languedoc-Roussillon

Vineyards and wine can be fashionable for a time and then fall away. During the 1970s, it was all Beaujolais. Then the reds of the Loire (Touraine, Anjou, Saumur) took over. Since the 1990s, it's been the turn of the Languedoc.

What sommelier, what wine waiter now fails to offer their more adventurous customers a red Languedoc? For example, I first tasted a Domaine de la Colombette at the "Atelier de Robuchon"—the wine was an athlete singing with the accent of its country. My guest had some in his cellar, but he didn't recognize it—entirely excusable in the foodie fever of a restaurant packed with diners. This local wine, a vin de pays from the Coteaux du Libron, has been anointed by Robuchon in person and thus at a stroke acquired a considerable hike in my buddy's consideration, and cellar.

In fact, nowadays, the entire Languedoc region is being promoted and recommended by Paris wine waiters, and deservedly so. Because the largest and oldest wine region in France (around Narbonne)—even if it continues to churn out ready drinking wines whose sales are plummeting because customers are becoming more and more choosy—is now competing with the best. Though it is not always doing so without some "new-oak" snobbery, fashionista enology, and prices that, here and there, make no sense. There was, there still is, a "rush" on Languedoc, just as there was a "rush" to the rivers of Colorado. And the majority of these "gold diggers"—who are committed, often at huge expense, to a quest for quality and originality (local wines with one or several vine types)—have succeeded. Similarly with winegrowers who have focused their activity on local Pays d'Oc varieties.

Languedoc, a "land of contrasts" (a cliché banned from all journalism schools!): on the one side, overproduction and outdated traditions live on; on the other, barriers are broken, and innovation, selection, and daring are the rule. Sumptuous Maury, mellow Banyuls: fortified *vins mutés* from Grenache. Frontignan, beloved of Colette, Rivesaltes, Saint-Jean-de-Minervois: sweetish *vins doux naturels* made from Muscat. The tastebuds of my youth recall them well. A Roussillon version of Proust's madeleine cake, perhaps (another cliché banned from journalism schools)?

The Loire Valley

Of all French wine regions, this is the most stretched out, the most varied, and the most original. Though, like the river in spate, it is difficult to control; but, like the same river, in fine weather it is serene, majestic, serpentine, peaceful. Quiet flows the Loire, and the vines that follow its course—divided into duchies and principalities—bear all the hallmarks of ancient "Doulce France." Each estate bears the name of a château: de Fesles, de Suronde, de Vaugaudry, de la Turmelière, des Noyers, etc. And yet, the glorious, historical châteaus of the Loire and its tributaries (Amboise, Chambord, Chenonceaux, Blois, etc.) ennoble no actual appellations. In Bordeaux, where shacks are on occasion dubbed "châteaus," such monuments to the glory of tourism and trade would never have been left without a wine label to stick on their turrets! Vine varieties have settled on the banks of the Loire, upstream from Nantes to Roanne, like tribes: Melon de Bourgogne, Naturalisé Muscadet, Gros Plant, Chenin Blanc, Cabernet Franc, Cabernet Sauvignon, Groslot, Chardonnay, Sauvignon, Malbec, Pinot Noir, Pinot Gris, Chasselas, Gamay, and so on.

It seems only logical that the province so often chosen as a residence by the kings of France for its *douceur de vivre*, (gentle way of life), has fostered—as if emulating the monarchy—a multiplicity of appellations, titles, fiefdoms, and estates, preferring, each according to their interest, either blending or a unique family. The vineyards of the Loire Valley are in the image of the Valois and the Bourbons: family trees and offshoots, heritage and etiquette, muddle and jumble, prestige and excellence, lords and gentry, all higgledy-piggledy.

I particularly appreciate those unctuous, sweetish grandees exalted by noble rot. The grapes of white Chenin, exposed to the Anjou sun and to the fog that rises from the confluence of the Layon and the Loire, produce delicacies with evocative names like Quarts-de-Chaume ("quarter-thatch") and Bonnezeaux. Following an Indian summer, a Coteaux-du-Layon too can lay in a surprise or two. Vouvray, Balzac's favorite white, is seigneur of Touraine. Always made with Chenin, a vine variety whose adaptability verges on the miraculous, Vouvray comes in dry, medium dry (*demi-sec*), medium (*moelleux*), dessert (*liquoreux*), and

Pages 138–39
Benefiting from a sea breeze, the vines of the Madeloc estate are planted in spectacular terraces that dive down towards the Mediterranean. A Roussillon wine, it bears the appellation of Collioure.

Facing page
The Ladoucette estate is the most renowned for Pouilly-Fumé in Pouilly-sur-Loire.

Facing page
The seahorse, emblem of Coulée-de-Serrant, features on every bottle of this dry white Savennières, which is grown in accordance with biodynamic principles.

Page 144
From its château, the emblem of Mouton Rothschild, chosen by Baron Philippe, looks over the serried rows of vines.

even semi-sparkling (*pétillant*)! All depends on the soil, exposure, year, winegrower, and market. The *demi-sec* I find a little mongrel (a thousand apologies!), a touch bubbly, a bit of a clown. I prefer it in its dry, elegant, and haughty bloom; or, better still, in the burnished gold and hedonistic savor of its old age, born in a year of royal sunshine, known as a "Louis XIV year."

To either bank of the eastern Loire, Sauvignon sires the white lords of Sancerre and Pouilly, populist aristocrats who stick a Revolutionary cockade in their cork, and who, far from their châteaus, voted for the king's execution. Pouilly even leaves behind if not a smell of actual burning, then at least one of smoke, of gunflint, that makes it enviably idiosyncratic. As for Sancerre, it is prepared to hobnob with a certain Chavignol, producer of succulent goat's cheeses called *crottins* ("droppings"). Both Sancerre and Pouilly-Fumé have been so won over to the cause of democracy that they have allowed the successful establishment, between Bourges and Vierzon, of two country squires of spotlessly white doublets: Quincy and Reuilly. At the tail-end of the Loire, where the country around Nantes already breathes Atlantic iodine and gazes down on the lighthouses in front of it rather than the châteaus behind, Muscadet douses lemony notes over islands of seafood.

But the finest dry whites of the Loire come from the lands of Good King René I, duke of Bar, duke of Lorraine, count of Provence, king of Naples and, more relevantly here, duke of Anjou, and the last to reign, with praiseworthy refinement, over a duchy then separate from France. To the *moelleux* of Layon he might add, even closer to his château, on the right bank of the Loire, the dries of Savennières. It is unlikely that the wine map around Angers now resembles what it was then. But no one disputes the venerable fame of two exceptional *grands crus* of Savennières: Roche-aux-Moines and, above all, Coulée-de-Serrant, so adored by Curnonsky, the French writer on gastronomy (1872–1956), that he placed it among the five best white wines in France (with Château-Chalon, Château-Grillet, Montrachet, and Yquem, no less).

It is surely only to be expected that the royalist Loire has bestowed on France more monarchist whites than socialist reds. The latter elect to be resident above all in the Touraine, at Chinon, Bourgueil, Saint-Nicolas-de-Bourgueil, a furlong or two from the châteaus of Azay-le-Rideau and Langeais. This is Balzac country. The land of Rabelais. For Frenchmen, the wine of Touraine is inseparable from the memory of these two immense authors.

Excellent wine generates enthusiasm. And whatever you do with enthusiasm is generally successful.

Baron Philippe de Rothschild

Red Wines of the Médoc

Readers are invited to pick up their favorite French wine encyclopedia and consult the list of red wines of the Médoc that earned their classification in 1855. Descending the Gironde from the left bank of the estuary they will encounter the Margaux appellation (twenty-one *crus classés* or classified growths, including one *premier cru*: (Château Margaux); then Saint-Julien (eleven *crus classés*); then Pauillac (eighteen, of which three *premiers crus*: Château Lafite-Rothschild, Château Latour, Château Mouton Rothschild); and, last but not least, Saint-Estèphe (five *crus classés*), with, set off to the side, the Haut-Médoc (also five). Grand total: sixty. Contrary to the commonly held opinion in Bordeaux, the country is actually not that easy for outsiders to find their way around in, since prestigious names are to be found rubbing shoulders with lesser-known ones. And yet villages too possess a number of growths that are classified on the famous list.

For a winegrower used to harvesting grapes on slopes, hills, and even mountains, the Médoc is simply flabbergasting. Usually growers say that it is facing the sun, on scarps, where the vinestock clings and has to fight its corner that the grape draws its legitimacy and extracts its substance. But here: altitude zero? A featureless plain? OK, I exaggerate: the commune of Listrac "towers" almost 150 feet (43 m) above sea level! The head positively spins! All in all, then, the Médoc has neither height nor slope, and yet it produces wines whose striking personalities are in inverse proportion to its lack of relief. But there is the water of the Gironde. It has been said that "the best vines look over a river." And then there is also the ocean, the warm current of the Gulf Stream, and an Atlantic meteorology neither too dry nor too drizzly, to which Cabernet Sauvignon, which takes its time to reach maturity, is perfectly adapted. There are the *graves*, too: alluvial deposits that apparently sheared off the Pyrenees and glided down towards the Gironde, the Dordogne, and the Garonne over the course of a few dozen million years.

In the end, it is the very poverty of its Tertiary soils that gives Médoc (as well as some other Bordeaux vineyards) its richness.

Communion Wine

Communion Wine

Once again we face *the* question: which wine? What color was the wine in the cup Jesus lifted at the table of the Last Supper? Was it white or red that he metaphorically transformed into his blood, just as he changed the bread into his body? Out of three Evangelists who refer to the meal on Maundy Thursday (the fourth, John, does not mention it), not one indicates the color of the wine that underwent transubstantiation. Bird brains! Historians and exegetes have sought to solve the enigma. In vain.

In terms of its color, red wine is obviously suited to stand for blood. Red blood, red Bordeaux. But the Eucharist is a beautiful and opaque mystery; only a secular logic would insist on identifying blood with red in such an obvious way. Among Catholics, altar wine is actually white (but red among the Orthodox, the Byzantine Church being more rationalist, perhaps?). But a priest who resorts to red wine for reasons of convenience, taste, or health neither lapses nor sins.

Curiously enough, canon law itself says nothing about the color of the wine, whereas it does indicate that it must be made "with ripe and fermented grapes" and that "boiling does not replace fermentation." The priest's obligation to say Mass with a decent wine is an admirable stipulation. "When the wine is sour or foul, the matter is invalid; if it is turning sour or foul, the matter is illicit." To use as sacramental wine an AOC, or even a great vintage, is thus not prohibited—far from it. The Cardinal de Bernis did not hold back: once asked why he opted for a rather fine Meursault, he answered: "Because I don't want my Creator to see me make a face when I perform Mass."

It was for reasons of management—to help the hapless sacristan—that, from the sixteenth century, red wine was gradually replaced by white. As everyone knows, red wine leaves tough stains, even on ecclesiastical linen. Its traces are conspicuous and woefully incompatible with the dignity of the office, whereas splashes of white tend to be discreet. Thus, pragmatism won out over symbolism, facility over a steep laundry bill. It was also only for practical reasons that among Catholics the practice of giving the faithful wine to drink at Eucharist fell out of favor.

Pages 146–47
An early morning fog hangs over the vines at Château Cos d'Estournel in the Bordelais. A red Saint-Estèphe listed among the second *grands crus* in the 1855 Classification.

Facing page
A chalice containing the wine of the Eucharist presented by an angel in this nineteenth-century painting by Sébastien Melchior Cornu for the chapel in the Élysée Palace.

Pages 150–51
The choirboys' mission in the sacristy is to fill the cruets, not to guzzle the wine. *The Priest's Wine*, by Demetrio Cosola, 1875.

During World War II, as a choirboy in the church in Quincié, I often had the responsibility before serving at Mass of filling the cruets: one with water, the other with wine. At that time, the Beaujolais region dealt only in red (the production of dry whites is still very much in the minority today, but it is on the rise). I remember that the priest, if he sometimes happened to use a red, had at his disposal bottles of white wine supplied to him by the local growers, or donated by their wives, assiduous attendees at Sunday service. It was a sweet tipple made from grapes forgotten by the vintagers or left on the stock because they were not ripe enough during the harvesters' first pass. The grapes of this aftermath were known as *"grisemottes."* They were not very productive, but there was enough to ferment a barrel of an unusual wine earmarked for domestic consumption—for vigils, in particular. Women were particularly fond of a tot as they sat knitting, while the menfolk, imbibers of red, played cards. I speak in the past tense because such vigils no longer exist, no more than the local white wine, nor *grisemottes* for that matter—except in those now infrequent years when the grape harvest is meager: 2003, for instance.

The water in the cruet has two functions: to purify the hands of the celebrant and to dilute the wine. Dilute it? At most to add a drop or two of water before it is consecrated. This is stipulated by canon law: "The quantity of water mixed with the wine must be very small," according to the Council of Florence: "A 'very small' quantity means that the nature of the wine should not be altered, something that obviously depends on the quality of the wine employed. A few drops of water suffice." I fondly believe that this addition of a dash of water to the wine is inherited from ancient Mediterranean civilization. Unless you wanted to pass for a "barbarian" (a redneck), in the Roman Empire, it was felt obligatory to dilute one's wine. More water is added to the sacramental wine among the Eastern rites of Christendom: among the Copts it's a third.

The Catholic Church has adroitly kept faith with these few droplets of water for their symbolic significance, for they represent humanity mixed with the blood of Christ.

One must try to be young like a Beaujolais
and age like a Burgundy.

Robert Sabatier, *Le Livre de la Déraison Souriante*

Facing page   A rare and little-known poster by Francis Bernard.
It is on view in the Hameau du Vin at Romanèche-Thorins,
which presents one of the most exhaustive collections of wine-related posters.

Vintages

An inscription on a Roman amphora translated by archeo-enologists attests to the oldest recorded vintage: the year 182 BCE. According to Pliny the Elder, the best in all Antiquity was the 121 BCE vintage. But 102 BCE was not bad either, especially the Falerne, when aged a good twenty years. Greeks and Romans considered that the best growths, like the wines of Sorrento, Chios, and Lesbos, had to wait ten to twenty-five years before being considered worthy of the table of the high and mighty. Amphorae containing wine that had been aged for a century or more were opened by "collectors" in Athens and Rome, but they left us no tasting notes.

Wine owes much of its prominence in *Realms of Memory* (an erudite exploration of French cultural heritage directed and edited by Pierre Nora) to the fact that notable vintages constitute fixed points in history, evolution, inconstancy, and popularity. After all, a remarkable year for wine represents a triumph over the weather. And people do not just mention or refer to fine vintages, they expand on them; since the wine in truly glorious bottles changes very slowly, opening out to attain a beauty and flavor at some indefinite time, sooner or later in the future, before declining like any sublunary living thing. Even if they are very old and become if not undrinkable, then at least disappointing and very different from what they once were, great bottles of exceptional vintages are genuine works of art. Collectors' items; witnesses to and protagonists in centuries of history; objects of financial speculation; sometimes patriotic relics.

The year 630 CE was a great year because a comet crossed the sky and the vines produced a vast abundance of grapes. At that time, a year was regarded as miraculous when yield was bountiful. Once again, in 1811, the wine of the comet was exceptional in both quantity and quality. Madame Clicquot had a special label made: "*Vin de Bouzy 1811 de la Comète.*" Moët et Chandon and other Champagne houses have employed the same USP. It is the star of 1811 that one can still see on certain labels, on Dom Pérignon in particular. Outstanding vintages of the twentieth century can clearly owe little to the stars, since the passage of Halley's Comet in 1910 and 1986 did not create bumper harvests (though 1986 Médocs are flatteringly pricey).

Facing page
Bottles of 1959 laid down in the cellars at Château Margaux. Exceptionally fine, this vintage has remained a benchmark after more than half a century.

Facing page
With Cassandre, Paul Iribe was one of the most important poster artists of the beginning of the twentieth century. The waiter is telling the diner that his guest (the wine) has been waiting for him for forty years.

Like their predecessors in the nineteenth century, the great vintages of the twentieth century were produced by a combination of the genius of the *terroir* with suitable climatic conditions that ensure (when they don't sabotage it) the vine's proper vegetative cycle. And lastly, they depend on the winegrower's labor, from pruning to bottling, not forgetting the supreme moment, the actual winemaking—a precarious exercise where nowadays science and technology allow more and more the production of the wine that the enologist planned and less and less that of the grower's intuition. In any case, no opulent harvest can ever occur without a regal sun in August and, especially, in September, when it should force grape-cutters to wear hats every day of the harvest.

In the "exceptional vintage lottery" of the last century (let's choose twelve figures out of a hundred), the numbers to go for would have to be the 1921, 1928, 1929, 1934, 1945, 1947, 1959, 1961, 1989, 1990, 1996, and the 2000. Bonuses for luck: the 1911, 1966, 1978, 1983, 1985, 1988, and 1995. If the experts agree on most of these years, others are debatable, depending on whether one is discussing Bordeaux, Burgundy, Champagne, Côtes-du-Rhône, or whatever. The sky does not vouchsafe its benefits uniformly. The years I mention are those in which the majority of French vineyards excelled themselves. Thus, in such a classification, it would be impossible to cite, for example, 1970 and 1975, which were dreadful for Burgundy, or 1997, rich only for the wines of the Loire. For the amateur, wine-sellers such as the Savour Club (www.savourclub.com) publish rather useful charts grading the years covered. Marks are allotted to each major area of production for each year. Comparison between such fatally subjective lists is the stuff of impassioned debate. I have had an enduring confidence in the vintage chart established by Jean-Claude Vrinat, manager of the Taillevent restaurant and founder of the cellar of the same name: it has never led me astray, though I can hardly forgive him for having ditched Beaujolais for the wines of Languedoc and Provence. It would have just meant an extra line! For the entire twentieth century he never awarded a single 19 (out of 20) to a red or white Burgundy—a supreme honor bestowed at least once since 1945 to every other major wine region. Red Burgundy had to wait until 2002 to have a 19. But was this actually its most deserving year?

Monks and Winemaking

Who, of the Benedictines or the Cistercians, were the more talented winegrowers? To whom, as a reward for their labor in earthly vineyards, would God in his heaven entrust the best slopes, those facing the eternal sun? If I had been a monk winegrower in the Middle Ages—and even before or afterward—would I have preferred, solely for the excellence of their wines, to toil under the lofty patronage of St. Benedict at Cluny (for the Benedictines) or at Cîteaux (among the Cistercians)?

If it is on record that the rules St. Bernard imposed on the Cistercian order were far tougher than those of the Benedictines, and that his monasteries, in terms of their interior decoration and austerity, reminded the friars that terrestrial life had more in common with dishwater than with a *premier cru*, nevertheless he did not prohibit either wine or vine. Severe though he may have been, St. Bernard was all too aware that man cannot live on prayer alone and that wine is a key component of Christology. Still, it is he who probably invented a piece of advice that applies not only to monastics: *Moderate bibendum est* ("Consume in moderation").

According to experts, we would be very disappointed by the wines that left storehouses in monasteries at that time, even those that were reputed the best. It is reckoned, for example, that the red Burgundies were pale, closer to what we call a rosé today. Clarets, as it were. And if I skate over the necessity felt by monk winegrowers inhabiting "disadvantaged" regions, such as Normandy, to aromatize their wines with herbs, fruit, or honey, or to temper them with milk, or pep them up with ewe's blood, this is only from Christian charity. These tastes are no longer ours; our enological science and art are a far cry from their elementary, rustic efforts; we require wine to be much more than a pleasant, refreshing, or inebriating beverage.

The monks would tend their vines between Prime and Vespers (early morning and sunset), looking after the wine as they did their souls. Hospitality professionals, they were acutely conscious that the generosity of their guests depended substantially on the quality of the wine served. In the Middle Ages, all monasteries nestled among vine groves. This is the main explanation

Facing page
A rotund friar with a ruddy face delights in the quality of the wine he is about to drink.

Pages 160–61
A fourteenth-century illumination showing a monk drinking from the cask.

for the presence of vineyards on land in England and in northwest France that is not ideally suited to them. Was plonk another means of earning indulgences?

But, in general, and according to the criteria of the time, the wine produced by monks was considered the best. Many friars were men of science who, like Dom Pérignon, invented techniques that improved the winemaking and the conservation of a product blessed by heaven above. The reputation of an abbey had as much to do with the quality of their wine as with the beauty of its architecture or the pious observance of its community. In terms of a monastery's public profile, vinous attractions could only be surpassed by a crowd-pleasing miracle. A monk might, of course, abuse the product of his toil. Countless illustrations show spherical brothers with rubicund faces and a salacious look in their eyes seated astride a barrel, or merrily around a table, in front of jugs and glasses being filled by a serving wench holding her skirts up in her other hand. The hail-fellow-well-met monk, tippler and keg-gobbler, swallower of casks, always ready to raise the elbow, albeit to the greater glory of God, is a stock figure in risqué—raunchy even—literature. The most popular is Friar Tuck, of Robin Hood's merry band; the funniest is Father Gaucher, so high-spirited that Alphonse Daudet and the prior exempted him from Mass to avoid hearing him strike up a drinking song halfway through; the booziest is the Friar in Chaucer's *Canterbury Tales*. And the most famous in France is Rabelais's Brother Jean de Entommeures, a devotee—like the bibulous Gargantua and Pantagruel—of the "Dive Bouteille," whose portrait in the classic translation by Sir Thomas Urquhart and Peter Anthony Motteux runs:

> *There was then in the abbey a claustral monk, called Friar John of the funnels and gobbets,* in French *entoumeures, young, gallant, frisk, lusty, nimble, quick, active, bold, adventurous, resolute, tall, lean, wide-mouthed, long-nosed, a fair despatcher of morning prayers, unbridler of masses, and runner over of vigils; and, to conclude summarily in a word, a right monk, if ever there was any, since the monking world monked a monkery: for the rest, a clerk even to the teeth in matter of breviary.*

No sooner has he been presented to the reader than Jean bursts into divine service, pouring out the wine and pitilessly eliminating a gang caught purloining grapes from the vine groves of the Abbey at Seuillé. Inebriated and grasping monks are plentiful in

Facing page
The Benedictine monk Dom Pérignon, to whom champagne owes so much, as depicted by the glassmaker Félix Gaudin. This masterpiece of stained glass is the property of the Moët et Chandon estate in Épernay.

later libertine, revolutionary, and anarchist writing, as well as in antireligious caricatures and broadsides. A sociologist would coolly observe that the number of alcoholic monks has in all eras been precisely proportional to the number of members of the clergy and nobility who were fond of the bottle. A moralist might opine that it was more excusable for monks, given that the majority would have been in permanent contact with a temptation that their toil and care would have only rendered more desirable. A bad historian (bad, because without evidence), but a wise psychologist, would conclude this chapter on ruddy-face monks with an affirmation to the effect that they were surely more numerous among the Benedictines than among the Cistercians, since the latter order was created precisely as a reaction against the decadent pleasure-seeking of the former.

If one cannot say who—of the Benedictines or the Cistercians—sanctified the best wines, the number and site of their vineyards do allow comparisons to be made, and even to see more clearly into a geographical competition that must have been diabolical on occasion. The two orders planted vines all over Europe, in particular in Switzerland, Germany, and Spain. It is in France that they spread the farthest and thrived the best. They are not often found in the Bordeaux region, more in the southeast, the valley of the Rhône, and in the Loire (Muscadet and Pouilly-Fumé to the Benedictines, Sancerre and Quincy to the Cistercians). Then they are omnipresent in Burgundy, with a clear advantage to the Benedictines, who arrived first and formed the earliest corporation of monk-winegrowers. In addition, they possessed the Mâconnais around Cluny, the vines of Vosne-Romanée (including what much later became Romanée-Conti), Pommard, Gevrey, Corton, Savigny, the Clos de Bèze, Santenay, etc.

The English historian Desmond Seward has drawn up an impressive list of Burgundian villages and vintages sanctified by the labor of the Benedictines. But the Cistercians don't come off so badly either. Judge for yourselves: Chablis, Meursault, Musigny, Clos de Tart, Bonnes Mares, and, above all, the property of Clos de Vougeot were all theirs. But, if one adds on the Benedictine side their garden, their monopoly, and their masterpiece—that is to say, champagne, and then the *vin jaune*, born from the viticultural genius of the Benedictine nunnery of Château-Chalon, it is only fair to award three Burgundy stars to the Cistercians, but four to their monkish rivals.

Good wine is a necessity
of life for me.

Thomas Jefferson

Enologists

These are the technicians to whom the vineyard owners entrust the winemaking process. The most demanding, the best enologists do not just turn up a few days before the grape harvest. They offer advice and perform analyses during the whole year, from sampling the soil to a final test tasting before the wine is bottled. Enologists (from the Greek *oinos*, wine, and *logos*, knowledge) are genuine scientists, doing research and undertaking experiments in vegetable physiology, vine biochemistry and microbiology, the chemical analysis of vines, and so on.

Enologists are serious individuals whose recommendations have done much to improve the quality of their specialty. It is through them that science degrees have made their way into wine vats and storehouses: they have cleansed them of folklore and guesswork. Their reputation adds to that of the wine and to its value.

In Jonathan Nossiter's documentary film *Mondovino*, the offhandedness and self-satisfaction of the character of Bordeaux enologist Michel Rolland gave the trade a bad name. He was quite unlike his predecessor, Émile Peynaud, who was confident in terms of the authority that his expertise and a wealth of experience conferred on him, but was also attentive, thoughtful, patient, and a good teacher. I once asked how he could act as enologist for such an impressive list of châteaus at the same time, even if, here and there, he would be consulted only for specific problems. Didn't his taste tend to make him reproduce the kind of wine he liked, and, even if variants and idiosyncrasies are unavoidable, to unify the flavor of "his" wines? Was there a "Peynaud taste," as there is today a "Rolland taste," which is the "Parker taste" (as *Mondovino* demonstrates)? Émile Peynaud answered that, though it's true he would never change his ideas and methods from château to château, and that top tasters with extremely perceptive palates might be able to recognize an "identical structure" in "his" wines, he had too much respect for the specificity of each wine to want to stifle it. He summed up his philosophy in one sentence: "In my vats, I have always tried to mix sufficient *spirit of finesse* with the indispensable *spirit of geometry*" (*Le Vin et les Jours*).

Page 164
A glass of red wine stands on the counter while a customer peruses the newspaper in a bar in the Saint-Paul district of Paris.

Facing page
A drawing by Dupuy & Berberian for Jonathan Nossiter's 2004 movie *Mondovino*.

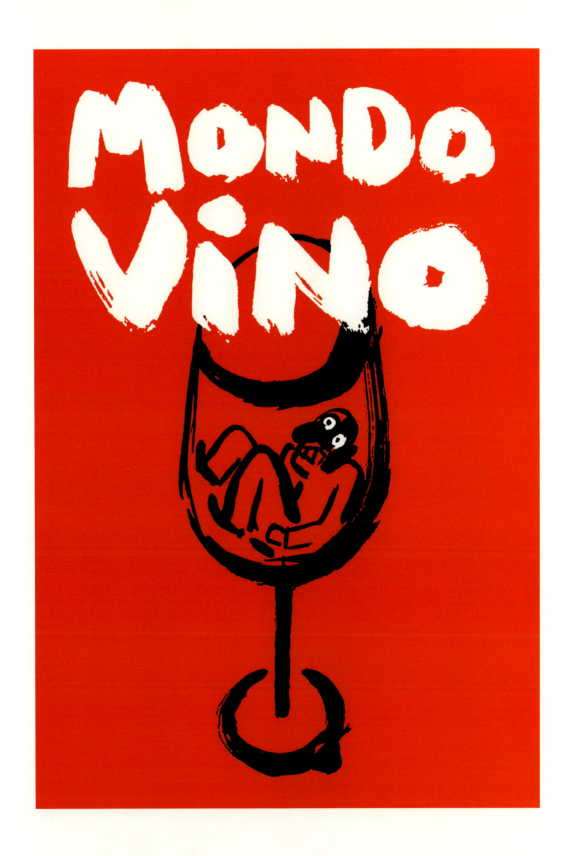

> Accept what life offers you and try to drink from every cup. All wines should be tasted; some should only be sipped, but with others, drink the whole bottle.
>
> Paulo Coelho, *Brida*

Pétrus

Like Burgundy's Romanée-Conti, Pétrus is a legend, a myth, a dream, a reference and a reverence, a revelation, and an *idea* of wine—a red utopia. For the majority, however, its very existence is just hearsay. And what do they "say"? They say that this Pomerol has, in the judgment of many international experts and in terms of worldwide notoriety and price, managed to supplant the great châteaus of the Médoc. They say that it has even indulged in the aristocratic luxury of excising its château's prefix to leave, not without pride, the plebeian abbreviation of Pétrus. They say that it owes its bouquets of unbelievable richness, its powerful, velvety sensuality, its princely roundness of palate to a bed of thick, unctuous clay mingled with a little sand where the Merlot (95 percent plus 5 percent Cabernet Franc) is as happy as a pig in mud. They say that the 28 acres or so (11.4 hectares) of Pétrus are picked solely in the afternoon, when the grapes have not a drop of morning dew left on them. They say that, with advice from the talented enologist Jean-Claude Berrouet, Jean-Pierre Moueix, and then his son Christian, they have introduced so many innovations and refinements to their winemaking that they have turned it into a work of art, the equal of those signed by Dubuffet, César, and Richard Serra that adorn their mansion.

Compared to its respectable, venerable cousins in the Médoc, Graves, and Sauternes, Pétrus feels almost nouveau riche. The twentieth century is its century; the nineteenth was theirs. Pétrus has ventured from Libourne to conquer America—but not the America of Jefferson, Rockefeller, and Henry James, but that of the Kennedys, Andy Warhol, and Truman Capote. "Pétrusians" affirm that, among other qualities, it is the very modernity of Pétrus—or rather a certain contemporary feel—that they appreciate. A fact belied by its rather tired label—though that, of course, is drunk only with the eyes. Could this be because Pomerol produces more sensual, less cerebral wines than the Médoc, the Graves, and Saint-Émilion, and that no one has had to wrack his brains to classify its growths? Nevertheless, there is an official classification, which, needless to say, Pétrus heads by a length.

Page 168
Bottles for Bordeaux, Burgundy, champagne... in every case, the wine keeps better in tinted glass.

Facing page
Unlike its famous Bordeaux neighbors, Pétrus is a quintessentially twentieth-century wine, though its peerless qualities place it high on the list for lovers of *grands crus*.

Pinot Noir

The vine varietal of Burgundy red. All alone, without swaggering, it produces a *jus* that changes into the little matter of Romanée-Conti, Chambertin, Volnay, Clos de Vougeot. In the race to the finest wines, the Pinot Noir of Burgundy (it is called *pinot* because it resembles a pine cone) carries off the champion's bouquet.

Let us list, rather too hastily, some of the finest creations from Pinot Noir in Burgundy (Romanée-Conti has an entry all to itself).

Chambertin. One occasionally used to see someone screw up their face at some foul wine and exclaim: "Well, that's no Chambertin!" The great vintage of Burgundy was then a watchword for a *grand vin*. If the expression is no longer current, Chambertin has kept a reputation as a magisterial Burgundy, with nine *grands crus*. It was also Napoleon's favorite wine (though he adulterated it with water). Chambertins resemble their name: ample, powerful, long in the mouth; increasingly complex and subtle with the years.

Chambolle-Musigny. This *commune* possesses a collection of the prettiest names for *climats*: Charmes ("Charms"), Derrière la Grange ("Behind the Barn"), Sentiers ("Paths"). One could write a novel featuring all these evocative names. *Bonnes Mares* ("Nice Ponds") is one of my favorite Burgundy *grands crus*.

Nuits-Saint-Georges. The Place du Cratère-Saint-Georges reminds one that an indentation in the Moon was baptized the St. George Crater by the astronauts of Apollo 15. This commemorated the bottle of Nuits that the heroes of Jules Verne's novel *From the Earth to the Moon* opened to celebrate their fictional success.

Pommard. Used to be written *Pomard*. The double "m" bestows a sturdiness, a tannic toughness to this wine from the Côte de Beaune. A wine of patience, sleep, comfort, and voluptuous pleasure, Pommard is like a big tomcat. You have to bide your time until he opens an eye and stretches out a paw.

Volnay. The village next to Pommard. They form a couple: Pommard, the male, and Volnay, his fiancée, all finesse and scents of fruits of the forest. But there can be a hint of femininity in a Pommard, while a few Volnays sprout hairs on their upper lip.

Pinot Noir may be a deadly earnest vine, but it is not above playing a few tricks.

Facing page
A bunch of pinot noir grapes, dense and closely packed, resembles a pinecone.

Provence

Of all French winegrowers, it is those of Provence, forced to expend all their energy in producing quaffing wines of character, who are the most deserving. It is so warm in Provence and the scenery so glorious. British wine journalist and expert Oz Clarke almost fell for the atmosphere of easy-living nonchalance: "Lazing in the shade before a bouillabaisse, some *aïoli*, and a mullet (what an appetite!), I've already felt my guard drop as I sipped a seriously chilled white or rosé and admired the shimmering sea, in such bliss that I lost all my critical faculties." Yet the latter made their presence felt, when, pulling himself together, Clarke thunders against the "heaving masses of pitiful rosés, whites without fruit, and emaciated reds."

But here, as in nearby Languedoc, young, ambitious winegrowers are adding wines of personality to the reputed products of traditional estates. It is now fun to devote a little time to choosing a red, a rosé, or a white from among the appellations Baux-de-Provence, Côtes-de-Provence, and Coteaux-d'Aix-en-Provence. There are numerous varieties, and there is more chance of unearthing buoyant, breezy examples exhaling delicate notes of scrub at the producer's than in the village mini-market.

Why did the authorities impose on the winegrowers of Pagnol (that's not an appellation you've never heard of; it's the author of *Jean de Florette*) such complicated and unbending rules of *assemblage* and therefore of varietal planting? For example, at Bandol (a place of appellation this time, not a writer, and the best, along with the three other AOCs: Cassis, Bellet, and Palette), white wine *has* to be made up of 60 percent Bourboulenc, Clairette, and white Ugni. For red Bandol, the law is stricter still: it is forbidden to add more than 15 percent Syrah and/or Carignan to the three obligatory varieties: Mourvèdre, Grenache, and Cinsault. Brussels, competition, the desire, and the drive to innovate—perhaps all these factors will force the authorities to loosen the straitjacket of wine regulation on grape varieties in such appellation areas.

Facing page
A rosé, a wine of sunshine and holidays, is best drunk lightly chilled in a shady garden. This Côtes-de-Provence will serve as a perfect aperitif.

Drinking good wine with good food in good company is one of life's most civilized pleasures.

Michael Broadbent

Grapes

It wasn't possible for Adam and Eve to be tempted by grapes since the vine had not yet been presented to humankind, or discovered. Therefore the forbidden fruit—symbol of prohibition, emblem of transgression, and crunchy representation of sexual temptation—had to be an apple.

A bunch of grapes, white or black, is significantly more sensual than an apple, though. Each berry is an invitation to indulgence. More than any other fruit, the flesh and juice of each tiny shining blond or bronze pearl, as it explodes on the tongue and oozes through the mouth, evokes the pleasures of the flesh. Old erotic drawings and photographs often show men squashing grapes over the cleavage or stomach of their mistress, whereas a lover peeling an apple in similar fashion is a rarity.

If apples are as round as breasts, the triangular form of a bunch of grapes is redolent of the female pudendum. A drawing by Barbe of a naked couple shows the female's pubic triangle replaced by some blond grapes, while a black bunch hangs upside-down over his erect penis. In French traditional slang, a *grappe* ("bunch") means the male sexual organs, while *pomme* ("apple") is just the head or face.

Today, the apple has been so thoroughly cleansed of its identity as a forbidden fruit that it has been chosen as an icon by the City of New York—and by Macintosh. Grapes, on the other hand, surface increasingly as an allegory of youth, sensuality, beauty, pleasure. Interior decorators paint orgies of grapes; likewise jewelers, textile and porcelain designers, and couturiers. There are no more forbidden fruits, of course; but the bunch of grapes, light or heavy, stylized or realist, has left the table or fruit dish of still-life painting and now symbolizes temptation. The adjectives applied to grapes seem tributaries of the language of eroticism: fleshy, pulpy, juicy, sticky; a prelude to the intoxicating overlap between words for the body and those for wine. A grape harvest may be an invitation to more than just picking grapes. Poor Adam! Poor Eve! Poor apples!

Page 176
"So numerous are the flavors among the enormous variety of wines that they can be seen as a kind of digest of Creation, a magic vessel containing the vastness and heterogeneity of Nature."
B. P.

Facing page
This trompe l'oeil bunch of grapes is a piece of virtuoso painting by Léopold Boilly, now hanging in the Musée des Beaux-Arts, Rouen.

Winegrowers' Rivalry

Burgundy vs. Champagne. Long before the reign of Louis XIV, a rival to Burgundy was on the up, making its mark to the north: Champagne. Medics quarreled—which was the better wine of the two for the health was a subject furiously debated in the neighborhoods of Rheims and Épernay with all the posturing and bluster of a weigh-in for boxers. The arguments presented by the sawbones from Champagne must have seemed both pointed and compelling, since they convinced the dean of the Hospices de Beaune to rush out a *Defense of the Wine of Burgundy against the Wine of Champagne*. But Fagon, Louis XIV's court physician, had resolved the dilemma by decreeing that the dropsy from which the king suffered could not tolerate champagne, whereas a Burgundy seemed to go down fine. Fagon's predecessors had been of the opposite view; Molière (1622–73) was already poking fun at the contradictory prescriptions of the doctors of his time. (Nevertheless, Fagon fully deserves the street in Nuits-Saint-Georges that bears his name.) There then proceeded to take place a classic winegrowers' set-to as Burgundy and Champagne each sought to obtain flattering notices from influential individuals (kings, princes, lords, dignitaries of the Church and the army). The equivalent today would be a battle between socialites waged in the media.

In all probability, competition between vineyards and wines started as soon as, somewhere in the Caucasus or Syria, there sprung up more than just one property and one winegrower. Having just concluded his census of the principal wines of Italy, Pliny the Elder (23–79 CE) wrote: "I am not unaware of the fact that the majority of readers will reproach me my many omissions, because each favors his own wine, and, wherever I go, it is always the same story."

Bordeaux vs. Burgundy. Pierre Veilletet, from the Bordeaux region himself, informs us that, on the banks of the Gironde, the Dordogne, and the Garonne, the most terrible anathema anyone can utter is "You... Burgundian!" In an interview in *Lire*, December 1986 (a magazine whose editor in chief I then was; you can see how tolerant I am), writer Philippe Sollers, born near

La Mission-Haut-Brion, could hardly contain his contempt for Burgundy: "I loathe it. It's a wine of sauce and blood. Just as, in the struggle between the Armagnacs and the Burgundians, I've chosen my camp, in the same way, in the literal civil war between the wines of Burgundy and Bordeaux, there must be no doubt as to the side I support. Still, people need to be told: the fact is that Burgundy is not a wine—it is liquid for making sauces. Moreover, when one drinks Burgundy one has the terrible feeling of drinking something that has bled, not to mention the appalling, palpable heaviness of the ground. So, for me, all those who like Burgundy (and Beaujolais too) are, at the end of the day, clots! I'm not going to pull my punches.... They're clots, I tell you, clots!"

The scorn poured on Burgundy (and on all other French wines, excepting champagne) by the lords of Bordeaux is a matter of record. Even if some writers on the review *L'Amateur de bordeaux* (Bordeaux Lover) at one time made staunch efforts to throw an olive branch over the border to Aquitaine, if one is from the Bordeaux region, one only drinks Bordeaux, one is interested solely in Bordeaux. One is born, lives, and dies in the religion of Bordeaux. A mono-enologist. A plonko-phobe. One may recognize, however, that Chardonnay has earned an eminent place for Burgundy in the white wine hierarchy. But it is among the reds that the noble, veritable battle takes place—or rather took place once upon a time, because that infallible and incorruptible taster, History, long ago decreed its judgment once and for all.

This is really no exaggeration. I have always been astonished by the lack of curiosity shown by Bordeaux fiends for other French wines, as well as for foreign products—except for those which, comprising Cabernet Sauvignon, Cabernet Franc, and Merlot, claim, in particular in California, to be able to compete with their models and masters—and which now can outdo them, even coming out top at blind tasting contests. As regards producers of Burgundy, there seems to be not so much an hostility to the wines of Bordeaux as an indifference. Or ignorance. They have no more doubt than Bordeaux makers that their wine is the best in the world (and in terms of white, they're right), but I have seldom observed scorn or intolerance among them. Perhaps they have the serenity of those who have become resigned collectively to being second-best, while the Gironde's superiority complex keeps on swelling. Should these contrasting attitudes (here given the broad-brush treatment, I admit) be seen as the result of the

Pages 180–81
Two great rivals, two mythical wines, objects of a genuine cult among buyers the world over: Romanée-Conti for Burgundy and Pétrus for Bordeaux.

Above
The label created by Jean Carlu in 1924 immortalized the ram, the emblem of Mouton Rothschild.

gustatory and psychological ascendency enjoyed by the wine of Bordeaux over all its competitors? Probably, yes.

It was England and Holland and then the United States that ensured Bordeaux's universal glory, hoisting it to first place in the hierarchy of wine regions of France and the world. The springtime gauging of the early *primeur* wine, for which lords of the manor in the Gironde invite international experts to their storehouses, has become an event almost as pulsating as the catwalks of haute couture. The comparison is not innocent. Just as few women are able to buy and wear the clothes on show, the finest Bordeaux can be acquired, and much later drunk and savored, only by a tiny, privileged minority, which paradoxically adds to the fame, and even to the popularity, of both Parisian couture and Bordeaux wine.

From *grands crus* to generic wine, Bordeaux has excellence, quality, diversity, and quantity—all the conditions necessary for punditry and pettifogging as well as for democratic consumption. Only champagne benefits from a comparable "impact," though of an entirely different nature.

Admittedly, Burgundy may flatter itself that it plays host to universally known villages and *climats* ennobled by the centuries. To fanatics from France and abroad, who bid for them to the stratosphere, it proposes bottles that are rarer than even the greatest Bordeaux. But its modest surface area prevents it from becoming sufficiently productive and diverse, as well as homogeneous in quality, to be able to reassert its long-lost sway over the market and taste.

Below
Meursault and Meursault-Charmes, two of the finest Burgundy whites.

Lastly, the wineglass is the theater of a clash between two civilizations. In one corner, the aromatic spontaneity of Pinot Noir, the fruity and floral explosion of its nose; and then its gradual transformation over time into a dazzling range of nuances into which the tongue delves. In the other, the impressive austerity of an *assemblage* dominated by the austere, "Jansenist" Cabernet Sauvignon, a base in which the best-honed palates can already distinguish—behind tannins that will temper over the years—the rotundity, richness, and finesse of tomorrow and, still more surely, of the day after tomorrow. On one side are the innate and the fundamental, all immediacy, tonicity, sensuality, straightforwardness; on the other are blending, expertise, patience, intellect, distinction, cosmopolitanism. Two philosophies, two cultures.

And all the pleasure resides in swapping glasses, in passing from the one to the other.

I'm looking for a wine that'll go well
with a piece of really, really, *really* bad news
I've got for my wife.

Facing page "Bad News," by Voutch, *Le Doute Est Partout* (Paris: Le Cherche-Midi, 2007).

Romanée-Conti

At the end of the very last broadcast of *Bouillon de culture* on June 29, 2001, I myself replied to the questionnaire that had so often been put to my prestigious guests over the ten years my arts program had been on the airwaves. The ninth question was: "In what plant, tree, or animal would you most like to be reincarnated?" My answer: "In a Romanée-Conti vinestock."

In my eyes, mouth, palate, and heart, Romanée-Conti is the finest wine in the world. It is, I conceded, not a particularly original choice. But it is hard to resist a legend when it is rooted in something so sublime. Not only does the jewel in the crown of the Côte de Nuits hold its own in the firmament of those few wines whose complexity and refinement are easier to eulogize than analyze, but every vintage adds to its mythical character.

For to partake of a Romanée-Conti is to dip one's lips in History. One is all of a sudden seated at table with Louis XIV, in Versailles. One is on friendly terms with Louis-François of Bourbon, prince of Conti, whose name is far better known for his purchase of Romanée than for his qualities as a military leader or his slanging matches with Madame de Pompadour. One joins in conversations with the functionaries of the Revolution, who confiscated the estate, but who also had the foresight to add for the first time the hated patronym of Conti to Romanée, as if sensing this might turn out a commercially profitable move. One walks through the village of Vosne to which another wily Burgundian affixed the name Romanée, the most prestigious vintage in the old village. One wonders how this 4½-acre (1.8-hectare) scrap of vine ever managed to attain global fame, and by what magic, through what grace, it manages, year after year, century after century, to grow masterpieces. Its limited size and yield make this wine scarce (6,000 bottles on average). Rarity and excellence incites desire. And exclusivity can only be had at a price. Its cost and scarcity mean that the miracle of drinking it comes along only once in a blue moon. The miracle reinforces the myth. And the myth adds to its splendor and reputation.

Romanée-Conti is the only wine that one cannot simply buy at the property, in single bottles or in cases of six or twelve. To enjoy the privilege of holding just one bottle, you have to place an order

Facing page
The cork in a bottle of Romanée-Conti is a tad longer than usual. Ensuring optimum conservation, it is synonymous with quality and longevity.

Pages 188–89
"One could read, engraved on a smooth stone: *Romanée-Conti*. Next to it, towering, majestic, the cross that has protected the vine since the eighteenth century. So, is it this square of vinestocks that is regarded as one of the treasures of the earth?"
B. P.

at the estate for thirteen to fifteen bottles: Richebourg, La Tâche, Romanée-Saint-Vivant, Grands-Échézeaux, Échézeaux—*premiers crus* all adjoining or close to the queen, and which are also hardly for everyday guzzling. Decades old, this kind of rationing may appear weird. But it is the only way, the only democratic way, of preventing the wealthiest snapping up the whole annual production and drinking it—or growing even richer by speculating on it. I've partaken of the legend on only five occasions, that is to say once every twelve years. That's not much, and yet, for the immense majority of Frenchmen who have never even tasted it, it's a lot.

Once, it was in positively criminal conditions, under the lights, on the overheated set of *Bouillon de culture*, in fall 1991. English author Richard Olney had published a dazzling, exhaustive tome on Romanée-Conti, on its history, owners, and the composition of the soil, on developments in growing techniques, vinification, and aging, on the vintages, and so on. Myths are all the more attractive when one can see them, or touch them, and, in this case, drink them. It was impossible to imagine the program without a bottle of Romanée-Conti being on the table, along with as many glasses as there were studio guests. But neither Richard Olney nor the estate had sent in a bottle. I possessed one, just one (a 1982), in my cellar, and thus it was "sacrificed." Under the harsh studio lighting, we savored it deferentially, commenting on it enthusiastically. But it was all over in a matter of seconds. It deserved more time, a thorough exegesis in a more convivial atmosphere. Family and friends reckoned I'd definitely taken professionalism a step too far.

Aubert de Villaine, joint owner and manager of the Romanée-Conti estate, once gave me a bottle—yes, absolutely: let the envious stop their ears; let tenders of the vine and the seraphim ring out together—a whole bottle of Romanée-Conti! The year? 1961. In his book, Richard Olney describes this classic vintage: "A peerless expression of the Romanée. Mahogany-colored *robe*. Gloriously dazzling nose mixing musk and spices, tremendous opulence in the mouth, comfortable and mellow enough to delight lovers of opulent Burgundies." That's just as well. I love an opulent Burgundy. I advise mistrusting opulence among humans and seeking it instead in wines. A wine, especially a red Burgundy, should not be born and brought up in poverty, cheeseparing and sallow. Nothing is too good for it, nothing ample or bold enough. It needs the company of rich wines, oozing with color and scent.

Pages 190–91
In order to ensure a measure of availability, the extremely rare Romanée-Conti is sold solely in cases together with other reds from the estate, each containing just one bottle of the fabulous wine.

Facing page
A detail from Caravaggio's *Bacchus*, used on the cover of a book by Kaiko Takeshi that tells the story of a Romanée-Conti 1935.

So here I am with a Romanée-Conti 1961 in my cellar, a bottle that now exists exclusively at the property or among a few collectors. But I am not a collector; I want to drink the thing. But when? With whom? I have a few ideas. I'm wary of engaging with a bottle in a slow-motion race that I might well end up losing.

The Japanese writer Kaiko Takeshi published a story set in Tokyo entitled *Romanée-Conti 1935*. One Sunday, in the winter of 1972, a novelist and a company boss chat away before a bottle of La Tâche 1966 and another of Romanée-Conti 1935. The company director knows France and its wines well, especially the Burgundies. He has traveled the "Route des Grands Crus" in search of great wines. He has visited the Romanée estate. He lunched at Chez Point in Vienne, spotting two bottles of Romanée-Conti from the mythical year of 1945. It is he who acquired the two bottles he is on the point of drinking with the novelist. The La Tâche 1966 is all youthful vigor. "Sensual opulence," writes Kaiko Takeshi, in the words of his businessman protagonist. But the Romanée-Conti 1935 is a cruel disappointment: watery, wilted, "a mummified wine."

Yet the Romanée-Conti 1935 drunk in 1991 by Richard Olney (note that our Japanese characters unstopped their bottle eighteen years previously) presented "a nose alive with clayey soil and wet thatch. Tobacco, Russian leather. A touch sinewy, solid in the mouth. Wonderful!"

How can the utter difference between two bottles be explained? Richard Olney's had never left the estate, whereas the Japanese's businessman's Romanée-Conti had transited through the United States before being packed off to Tokyo. Perhaps it was the war that killed it off? "Having been thrown about and harassed, steamed in the summer heat, piled up, stored out in the sun, in the wind, left for dead, was the wine entering a premature senility?" the businessman wonders. All too likely.

My bottle of 1961 will not be subjected to the outrage of a long, uncomfortable journey or brutal storage conditions. It will surely be excellent. Moreover, Kaiko Takeshi's pen has his Tokyo businessman tell us that: "According to what I was told at Romanée-Conti, the wine of '69 has attained great maturity. That of '65 continues to grow. The '61 is perfection itself; all one can do is admire it." Sounds promising!

There are five reasons
for drinking: the arrival
of a friend, one's present
or future thirst,
the excellence of the wine,
or any other reason.

Latin proverb

Saint Vincent

The patron saint. A Spaniard, he had no links with winegrowing through his family or during his life as a deacon in Saragossa. It has been suggested that he owes his intoxicating glory to his martyrdom. The proconsul Dacian, Emperor Diocletian's right-hand man, condemned him, among other delights, to have his body pounded and crushed, until the blood spouted out like grape juice under the impact of a press. The metaphor is unforgiving, especially for people as generally cheerful as winegrowers. Sewn into an ox's skin, Vincent's corpse was then thrown into the sea off Valencia. By one of those miracles that have tended to die out in our age, by the time the oarsmen got back, his sacred remains were already waiting on the seashore.

This victory over the salty waters should surely have made Vincent patron saint of sailors and the shipwrecked? Yet, rather than water, he was allotted wine. He seems to have been luckier posthumously than on earth. His rewards went further: Vincent is the patron of winegrowers, merchants, and inspectors, of enologists and wine-bar owners. As well as of vinegar manufacturers. So, however good or bad a year might be, someone will always light him a candle.

It is perhaps in Paris that one might unearth the explanation for the saint's "career change" to winegrowing. The body of the Iberian martyr was dispersed in the form of relics, and his tunic and one of his arms ended up in an abbey built by King Childebert I in the capital; it was duly consecrated as Sainte-Croix-Saint-Vincent. And, as the abbey possessed many vines in Île-de-France, the monastic winegrowers chose St. Vincent as a rampart against frost and hail. His cult then extended to other vineyards. Three centuries later, the relics of another saint, Germain, supplanted those of Vincent, and the abbey changed its name to Saint-Germain-le-Doré. Then, later still, Saint-Germain-des-Prés. In a de-Christianized France, St. Vincent is still a household name. He is one of the few saints who continue to spark enthusiasm, prayers, and processions—either on his saint's day, January 22, or else during the following weekend. It is in Burgundy that he is celebrated the most. The tribute is first Christian (procession, solemn mass, sermon, blessing), then secular (banquet, trip round

Page 194
Elliott Erwitt likes to take photographs of everyday scenes from curious angles, as with these wine glasses on the terrace of a Parisian bar.

Facing page
In Burgundy, St. Vincent, patron saint of winegrowers, is celebrated in a different village every year. This statue is on show in the Hameau du Vin, Romanèche-Thorins.

Saint Vincent

Facing page
The Virgin Mary, protector of the grape harvest, here depicted by Pierre Mignard as *The Virgin of the Grapes* (1640–50) in a painting in the Louvre.

the cellars, exhibitions, folksongs, and so on). Let's just say that the morning belongs to St. Vincent and the remainder of the day to Bacchus. This alliance between the religious and the pagan comes from the Middle Ages. The formula pronounced by the Grand Master of the Brotherhood of the Knights of the Tastevin at his enthroning mentions Noah, "father of the vine," and Bacchus, "god of wine," as well as St. Vincent, "patron of the winegrowers." Such broad ecumenism is preferable to the war that used to break out in some Burgundian villages in the late nineteenth century, with a clerical procession, complete with banners and hymns, and another, anti-clerical, with flags and the Marseillaise. Two rival banquets then followed. It must have been a riot.

The Burgundian Saint-Vincent celebration is known as "turning," because it is held in a different village each year. It is an occasion for all the other wine guilds of the region, trade associations, and cultural bodies to send delegations; they take up their seats behind a statue of the patron saint carved out of the wood from an old vine-press. This is then paraded to the sound of a band by the members of the Great Council of the Brotherhood of the Knights of the Tastevin in full regalia. They then proceed—and this is the sweetest and most emotional moment of day that is both freezing (it's late January) and warm (everyone drinks to keep out the chill)—to enthrone the village's oldest winegrowers of both sexes.

The patron saint's rivals. Saint Vincent hasn't had it all his own way. He has had numerous competitors in France. The most often invoked is Saint Vernier, represented with a vintager's billhook in hand, since he was actually the son of a vintner and a grower himself. There is also Saint Martin, who had a donkey that invented pruning by grazing the vine, as well as Saint Urbain, Saint Marcellin, Saint Remi, Saint Blaise, Saint Antoninus, Saint Genevieve, Saint Hune in Alsace, and Saint George in the Mâconnais. It's amazing that the warm breath of all those guardians doesn't keep the frost and hail off the vines altogether.

Last but not least, the Virgin is readily invoked. Painters and sculptors often represent her with the Baby Jesus on her knees, with one of them holding in their hand a bunch of grapes. The festival of Mary falling on August 15, just as the grape begins to acquire its color, she was often called upon to protect the harvest by way of symbolic gestures and manifestations of piety.

Drink wine. This is life eternal.
This is all that youth will give you.
It is the season for wine,
roses and drunken friends.
Be happy for this moment.
This moment is your life.

Rubáiyát of Omar Khayyám

Facing page A decanter is used to let red wine breathe and so bring out its flavors.

Wine and Sex

Here's Noah, tipsy, his privates exposed to the view of his sons: sex didn't wait long to enter into a scandalous relationship with wine. Both give pleasure to the point of unhinging the senses. Both are intermittent pleasures: one provides it in gulps, the other in jerks. Past masters at sparking internal quiverings, wine and sex have been transgressing together since time immemorial. Their complicity dismays bigots and hypocrites, and upsets the prim and the prudish, who are revolted by these partners in crime.

Every civilization of the vine has celebrated Bacchanal eroticism in its art. Babylon, to start with, where drinking bouts and scenes of sodomy alternate on buckets and vases. Artists, whether Greek, Etruscan, or Roman, vied with one another in depicting love scenes and saucy, even pornographic, pictures on utensils used for wine: krater, amphora, cup, and kylix. Paintings could also (as in the frescos of Pompeii, for example) give drinkers ideas—especially if prostitutes were invited to their libations. Later, screenwriters saw fit to saddle Cesar Borgia with a timeworn erotic fantasy: red wine is poured over the white, naked bosom of a woman for him to lick off. During the orgies held by Barbarians, or by monks, the first thing to be penetrated was a barrel. Before the "seminal fluid," it was the wine that ran in torrents. Unlikely in such circumstances that guests would take the time to discuss the *robe*, the *length*, the *legs* of a wine. It is not difficult to guess how, in the erotic language of wine, if a wine has *"corsage,"* then it smacks of the feminine and the plump. This *odor di femina* derives from fantasy foreplay, from the oceanic alteration of a fortified wine.

If wine stimulates the libido of man and woman alike, emboldens them, warms the blood and the tail, drunk in abundance it is more liable to lead to slumber than to copulation. As we read in classic accounts of marital fiascos, where the young groom, without even the strength to undress, spends the wedding night in the conjugal bed snoring like a foghorn. Except for rare exceptions, a drunk, or even a man just a little the worse for wear, does not make a good lover. Two glasses, and we're off; three and you're asking for trouble! As in all human activities, the greatest variation and thus injustice reign in men's ability to enjoy—at the

Facing page
The Bottle Walking the Streets, a work by Michel Tolmer, whose drawings are exhibited in a number of good Paris wine bars, like the 6 rue Paul-Bert.

Pages 204–5
Claudia Schiffer photographed by Karl Lagerfeld for Dom Pérignon.

Facing page
A sensual and disconcerting scene showing a father, plied with drink by his daughters and succumbing to their attentions: *Lot and His Daughters*, by Simon Vouet, 1633.

same time or one after the other—both alcohol and sex. As the years draw on, the two devils become increasingly less compatible bedfellows. Drink *or* have sex. There's a time for everything. Wine maintains one in a state of appetite and of sensuality; sex makes one hungry and thirsty.

Nobody has described the physical battle between alcohol and the libido better than Shakespeare. We are in *Macbeth* (Act II, Scene 3). The gatekeeper, invited to a wedding the previous day, has been snoozing. Macduff, who has an audience with the king (whom he will discover a few seconds later has been assassinated during his sleep), is at this point still in the mood for banter. He asks the porter: What three things does drink especially provoke? Porter: "Marry, sir, nose-painting, sleep, and urine. Lechery, sir, it provokes, and unprovokes: it provokes the desire, but it takes away the performance. Therefore, much drink may be said to be an equivocator with lechery: it makes him, and it mars him; it sets him on, and it takes him off; it persuades him, and disheartens him; makes him stand to, and not stand to; in conclusion, equivocates him in a sleep, and, giving him the lie, leaves him."

Might this be bitter experience talking, Will?

The Bible is informative as well as pragmatic on the subject of the alliance between sex and alcohol. A widower, the aged Lot, three sheets to the wind, is raped by his two daughters during his sleep. Double ejaculation. Nine months later, he's a grandpa twice over. Nice work, girls! Abraham's nephew was clearly a sturdy devil and he deflates the argument of Plutarch and sundry other physiologists who contended that a drunk's seed flows in no more than feeble spurts and that its substance is poor and unlikely to inseminate.

The fact remains that many a mature man has come a cropper in the bed department after trying to affirm his virility by too arrogant an absorption of wine at table. Face to face with a woman, who would in the past have been forbidden alcohol and who today might like a drink or two, a man tries to demonstrate a seductive stamina by expounding on châteaus and pouring their produce with panache. A *grand cru* will, he reckons, afford *him* added tannin, savor, character—in short, *body*. He's got a bottle in, but not just any old plonk: *premier cru*, top dollar; the best. Let the woman he has in his sights make no mistake: she'll be going to bed with a great AOC, an exceptional, if late, vintage.

With the same, often unconscious, intention to parade their manliness through the intermediary of wine, other men adopt the reverse strategy: a modest appellation, from where they have managed to unearth a rarity, something sublime, known only to a handful of initiates. This will be a wine still young, natural, unfiltered, bursting with fruit and yet full of nuance and distinction: Don Juan pours his self-portrait. If his pretty guest does not feel like seeing, like tasting what's what, then it can only be because she's made of the same dull stuff as earthenware water-jugs. For a first date, rich, powerful, sunny wines, like a Côtes-du-Rhône or a Languedoc—wines that chef Alain Senderens dubs "ballsy"—cannot be recommended. That would be to raise the bar a mite too high.

Women who like to drink wine, who know about it, and who have even become experts, are increasing in number. From estate to restaurant cellar, competent and authoritative women are to be found working in every aspect of wine. A man would be ill advised to attempt an enophilic seduction of a woman he scarcely knows: today, she might well be better informed about the subject than him. Now, that *would* be a blow to his virility. There remain a few male drinkers who like to grumble about the irresistible rise of females in the footsteps of Bacchus. Admittedly, there are no longer many guys who subscribe to the old Lyon proverb: "For wine to do good for women, it should be the men who drink it" (in *La Plaisante Sagesse lyonnaise*). Still, since Antiquity, wine has been a man's business. Through it, men express their strength, their superiority, their domination, their sexism. Even drunkenness was a virile prerogative. For women, inebriation brought shame, dishonor, scandal. Today still, this may cause indignation and contempt. In short, women are to be found on winegrowing properties, in storehouses, cellars, merchants' firms, restaurants, bars, and working on wine-related Internet sites, and for specialist reviews. Often endowed with a more sensitive palate than their male counterparts, they have learned how to taste, spit, drink, compare wine, and to talk about it. Still nowhere near parity, they have quietly settled into the landscape. The men of the glass and the cork no longer have exclusive use of the corkscrew.

Facing page
Georges Barbier was a celebrated painter and fashion designer. He produced illustrations for several editions of Baudelaire, Musset, and others, and here, in 1928, for Paul Verlaine's *Fêtes Galantes*.

Sommeliers

Elsewhere in this volume I gently mock the jargon and verbosity of certain sommeliers. But I know many are extremely competent and wear their knowledge lightly. And some, the finest sommeliers in France (very good), in all Europe (formidable), and the whole world (unbelievable), are men to whom one can raise a hat, and then a glass. Predominantly men. Few women venture into the ring, though Anne-Marie Quaranta as early as 1980, Marlène Vendramelli in 1993, and Giovanna Rapali in 2001 have all won the trophy for best young sommelier in France.

Six Frenchmen have been awarded World's Best Sommelier: Jean-Luc Pouteau (1983), Jean-Claude Jambon (1986), Serge Dubs (1989), Philippe Faure-Brac (1992), and Olivier Poussier (2000). It would only be fair to add an Italian from Paris to this list: Enrico Bernardo (2004). The knowledge that they all had to expound upon, in written and oral examinations, extended to every vineyard and wine on the planet, and also covered a thousand other related subjects, such as geology, chemistry, cuisine, wine regulation, and more. The test demands years of solitary toil. And then there's the daily training in tasting wines—in analyzing, gauging, comparing, and recalling them—with the aim of winning the blind tasting, an exercise followed by the task of choosing the wines, whose identities they hope they've guessed correctly, to go with certain dishes, sauces and spices, as well as with a chef's or jury's surprise or two.

And what instruments does this marathon require? Oh, just a painter's eye, a botanist's nose, a squeaky clean palate, and the memory of a historian. A champion sommelier must recall the taste of all the thousands of wines that pass through his mouth once, thrice, ten times. Like a pianist, every day a sommelier practices his wine scales over and over again: spitting, noting, smelling, tasting, and, from the top, spitting.... This aptitude, this gift—their gift for wine—has to be kept up, worked at, maintained.

They do need a gift for words—but neither too many, nor too few. It's important to express the key elements in the words of their tribe, but what they say must also be clear enough to be understood by the average drinker.

Facing page
At a blind tasting held during the World Sommelier Championships in Athens in 2004.

People spend too much time tasting wine; not enough time drinking it.

Andre Tchelistcheff

Brotherhood of the Knights of the Tasting Cup

In France there are an enormous number of brotherhoods and confraternities established to celebrate a product, a dish, a saint, or a tradition. They meet up, wear special clothes, award ranks, throw press conferences, elect masters, swear allegiance, drink, eat, and fix another meeting for a new get-together celebrating the virtues of onions, cider, fancy Bresse poultry, handmade *andouille* of Guéméné, or pipes by the masters of Saint-Claude. Such *confréries* are especially widespread among wine lovers. Perhaps only because winegrowers, naturally high-spirited, communicative by temperament, traditionally sociable, enjoy the party atmosphere that is created when people drink their wines. A few well-chosen words of welcome, a little solemnity when tasting, and hey presto! annointed by Bacchus, St. Vincent, or the blessed entity that lent its name to the vineyard, you have new adherents dedicated to an AOC, a local wine, a variety, a tun, or a still— jolly drinkers and neighborhood soaks all!

The whole art of the larger brotherhoods—which were created, after all, to publicize their wine—is to make the people waiting to join forget the commercial reasons for their existence.

Since its creation in 1934, after years of poor sales for Burgundy, the success of the "Confrérie des Chevaliers du Tastevin" ("Brotherhood of the Knights of the Tasting Cup") has never been surpassed, probably because each "chapter" (around twenty or so meetings a year, with 550 diners packed into the Cistercian wine store in the Château of Clos de Vougeot) is at the same time ceremonial and popular. There is nothing uptight or off-putting about the event, in spite of the blast of horns, the crimson robes with gold facings worn by the dignitaries, all "Grand" by title (Master, Chamberlain, Constable, Seneschal, etc.), their faces impressed, some with stagey dignity, others with unfeigned joy. That's what's amazing about them: they make themselves serious enough for princesses, Nobel Prize laureates, and company heads to agree to be inducted, and yet remain sufficiently unfussy and Burgundian in mood for the dinner to be a junket at which even the members of the "Great Council" join in the fun.

Page 212
A row of glasses stand ready for a tasting. Some of these events have attained legendary status: on March 28, 1991, forty-four vintages of Romanée-Conti were uncorked in a single day.

Facing page
A bottle of Gevrey-Chambertin with the ribbon of the Confrérie around its neck, during the "Chapitre de la Musique" at the Château of Clos de Vougeot, in 2011.

216

Brotherhood of the Knights of the Tasting Cup

Corkscrews

No one knows exactly who invented the corkscrew, but he was probably English. The brainwave was inspired not by bottles of wine, but of cider. Was he native to a county where the hog was plentiful? The "worm" takes the form of a pig's tail, and it is the tail wagging the dog when we talk about the pig's "corkscrew tail."

It is in any case undeniable that it was a London clergyman, Samuel Henshall, who, in 1795, took out the first patent for what was already a sophisticated artifact, since it was equipped with a button. The English continued to innovate in the matter of corkscrew shapes, altering, varying, and improving the mechanism. During the nineteenth century, they lodged hundreds of patents, justified by tiny differences. It's only natural that the English genius should toil without stint to improve lawns, trenchcoats, rugby, and democracy. But why the corkscrew? Did the British feel morally obliged to bring to the great cause of wine, through an improved technique for opening the bottle, something they could not hope to bring to the art of filling the thing? Did it stem from a will on the part of consumers to get to the wine as quickly as possible, yet elegantly and safely too? Bernard Watney and Homer Babbidge do not explain this DIY passion for the corkscrew on the other side of the Channel. I note, however, that one is English and the other American, and that they are the authors of a tome (*600 Corkscrews for Collectors*) that has become the reference on a subject where one might have wanted the Greeks, the Italians, and the French (seniority *oblige*) to have manifested greater creativity. Perhaps we French allow the British precedence in this area in accordance with Count d'Anteroche's quip to Lord Hay at the Battle of Fontenoy: "Gentleman, we never fire first. After you!"

Having hailed John Bull's starring role in the history of the corkscrew, it should be observed nonetheless that the rest of Europe has not sat about twiddling its thumbs. Experts on the subject have identified practical, and especially artistic, specificities in Germany, Holland, Italy, and France (the Americans only got going later). French eighteenth-century corkscrews, if they do little more than adopt English techniques, may reasonably claim a status as works of art, the handle, the shaft, and the tip of the "worm" being made of silver, gold, or vermeil.

Pages 216–17
The dignitaries of the Confrérie during the "Chapitre de la Saint-Vincent Tournante," amid the vines of Chassagne-Montrachet, in 2010.

Facing page
Nineteenth-century print. "Great bottles do not like quiet corkscrews. Their apotheosis should make a bit of a racket!" B. P. (from *Les tweets sont des chats*).

If the French best demonstrate their inventiveness and talent in the pocket corkscrew, this does not prevent Her Majesty's staff as well as picnickers in Oxford, Eton, and at Glyndebourne, slipping penknife contraptions stamped *Made in England* into the hamper, beside bottles of the best Bordeaux.

I contend that the corkscrew, quite apart from its utility, is a most extraordinary household article. More than three centuries after its invention, it continues to stimulate the imagination of industrialists and craftsmen. I give you the spectacular "screw-pull," a cumbersome if highly effective machine (though to be avoided in the case of very old corks). It was created by Herbert Allen, an engineer with NASA. Goodness, between a module to fly to Mars and a capsule off to Pluto, at NASA they find time to bother with a thingummy designed for the cellars of Napa Valley!

It would take several pages to simply enumerate all the variants, additions, brainwaves, and stratagems, including on the shape of the prong, that Reverend Samuel Henshall's successors have brought to the corkscrew. Let's mention a few: they can be fitted with "wings" that are pulled back, or a propeller-screw, a release button, a (single or double) lever, a winch (no, really), a zigzag mechanism that opens like a concertina, etc. The diversity of handles alone, for practical or aesthetic reasons, is infinite. A familiar instrument, the corkscrew remains something enigmatic.

It has even earned a museum of its own in Ménerbes in the Luberon, holding more than a thousand corkscrews of all the aforementioned species, from all over the world and from every period. It is amazing how this tool has been combined with so many other articles and instruments: cigar-cutter, pipe-cleaner, lighter, scissors, snuffbox, bottle-opener, knife, spoon. At least these are all linked with the pleasures of the mouth. Others are even more unexpected: bodkin, tie-pin, cane, climbing piton, screwdriver, razor ("a tot while I glide it over your neck, sir?"), dagger, pistol, etc.

The travels of the corkscrew remind us that, without such a contraption, there's many a slip 'twixt cup and lip. My preferred corkscrew is the simplest: with a round, wooden handle and a twisted, pig's-tail worm. It requires one to hold the bottle tightly between the thighs and give it a strong pull. The promising pop of the cork as it is expelled from the neck is well worth the energy expended. But, as one ages, silent and less labor-intensive corkscrews are not without their advantages.

Facing page
To open this bottle of Loire Valley wine, nothing is more effective than a traditional corkscrew with a vinestock handle.

Barrels

The poet and one-time cooper Pierre Boujut (*Célébration de la barrique*) (Celebration of the Barrel) is right to note that the wine barrel was "a ludicrous, burlesque, counter-intuitive, unreasonable, anti-utilitarian invention. How could anyone have imagined storing liquids in a wooden contraption so difficult to build?" Essentially just wooden planks of curved form (staves). Who had the absurd but brilliant idea of the barrel?

Ancestors in Gaul. Pierre Boujut thinks that the Greeks and Romans were too serious to have dreamed up something so utterly whimsical. The amphora, the wineskin: these are practical, rational, reasonable! Only a population of pipe-dreamers and dilettantes could invent the barrel.

Celts were poets. On sculptures and bas-reliefs from the age of Caesar, ringed wooden barrels are shown lined up on boats. They were probably not made of oak, but appear of similar size to French *barriques*: holding around 57–61 gallons (215–230 liters). They look as if they come from the same cast (the French even say "barrel"). The famous barrel of the Danaides, on the other hand, was probably just a giant amphora. It is probable that Diogenes, who was born three centuries before Julius in Greece, a country that, because of the heat, long preferred the immutable ceramic of the amphora to the capricious timber of the keg, did live in a barrel. Robert Sabatier, however, who composed a brilliant five-hundred-page verse dialogue with the philosopher (*Diogène*), is inclined to see this as a legend. Still, he was quite within his rights to use it and suggest that Diogenes's barrel, his "rolling house," would have stunk of sour wine.

In France larger barrels were long employed as shelters for paupers and vagrants. Sizeable, standing upright and open wide, in Paris and in other cities they also served as improvised shopfronts for hawkers, darning-women, fortune-tellers, and three-card-trick merchants. And for public scriveners too. I like the idea that a tubby *barrique*, a *muid* from Burgundy, Roussillon, or Languedoc, a *pipe* from Anjou or Cognac, a *tonneau* from Bordeaux, or a *queue* from Paris—having once contained wine,

Facing page
The aging room at Château Beychevelle in the Bordelais, a *grand cru classé* of Saint-Julien, is open to the public and holds tastings.

perhaps delicious and expensive—might humbly end its days as a desk for a scribe writing letters for the illiterate. A less attractive extension of its use was commonplace in The Netherlands and in other countries of northern Europe: the barrel pillory. This was a keg in which women convicted of adultery would be locked for two hours with only their heads sticking out. Unable to either sit or stand, if her legs gave way, the half-squatting unfortunate would choke.

To this instrument of torture, allow us to prefer a "conversational convenience," a historical seat of French *esprit*, the *tonneau* or "barrel," in which Horace Walpole's friend Madame de Deffand held court. This was the name given in her salon to the armchair with a "barrel roof," in which the renowned blind bluestocking would converse with the greatest intellects of her age.

As a boy on vacation, I was often woken up by the sound of a vintner shunting barrels about the courtyard above a manhole and washing them out. Rolling an empty firkin required little effort. Still, to grip each end and lift them up, tipping them first one side, then the other, and at the same time to spin them, or to scrape the inside with a big chain, and then rinse them out—that was a man's job. I was just a kid whose arms were not long enough. Every year, my fruitless attempts were observed with amusement by Julien Dulac, the winegrower. Inevitably, he put my failure down to my not eating enough soup. Soup was performance-enhancing fare (that didn't worry me; I liked it), and I counted on its arm-lengthening, rather than height-increasing, virtues. I knew I was a man, if not yet quite barrel-chested, when I had enough arm-span and strength to hump a Beaujolais *pièce* of more than 57 gallons (216 liters) around without groaning.

"Woody notes" are all the rage with American consumers. They appreciate the concentrated, vanilla wines obtained by aging in oak casks. Or by the maceration of oak chips thrown into stainless-steel, steel, or concrete tanks (a process still prohibited in France but authorized in the New World). Is the result the same, using cheap chips and genuine yet costly barrels? I have my doubts. Pushy, crude, this oaky taste is a fashion that will pass, like all fashions. There will be a return to fresher, honest-to-goodness wines, in which the natural fruit predominates. Meanwhile, remember Jacques Puisais's killing little remark: "Here's a wine with more of the forest in it than the vine."

Facing page
In the Bordelais, the barrel room at Château Clos Saint-Martin, a Saint-Émilion *grand cru*.

Barrels

The sun, with all those planets revolving around it and dependent on it, can still ripen a bunch of grapes as if it had nothing else in the universe to do.

Galileo Galilei

Grape-picking

Paradise. I've never been at a grape harvest where I didn't fall in love. At twelve, fifteen, eighteen, twenty, it was always the same story. Each time I entered the vineyard to plunder, pillage it, my heart beat faster. So much so that, even today, in the fermentation room and leaning against a hand-press left out of nostalgia, or gazing at a watercolor by Dunoyer de Segonzac showing a grape-picker and two trug carriers gliding about the vines, I feel the warmth, the sheer pleasure rise anew. It is useless for my one-time companions of those nippy mornings and rainy evenings in September to try and remind me of numb and gashed fingers, of the too-heavy vats, of the gnawing fatigue caused by the ceaseless repetition of the same actions, of the temptation, faced with endless vines creaking with fruit, to throw in the towel. It's pointless telling me that it was a lot of work, a lot of pain. Because, for me, the weather was always fine, I was in love, and the grapes left their sugar on my lips.

In our day, youth was very constrained. The grape harvest felt like an interlude of freedom. It was there that I first earned some money. We were finally regarded and treated like adults. Before skulking back to school, before returning to the strictures of family life, we gamboled about in the vines like sparrows! For those who had an appetite for it, harvest-time was like a glorious school of sensuality. Hands stole round the stocks, glided over the leaves, slipping, shifting, seizing, and returning with heavy bunches of dew, sun, and juice. There was that feeling of plenitude that such bounty brings. There were cheeks smeared with grape juice (as red as a dyer's stain), fingers sticking to the apron or the trousers, the skin soiled, roughened, and deliciously rank. There were wasps, driven crazy by the vats and bucket-chain, drunk and ravenous, which claimed their share, and which, in the afternoon heat, rendered our ransacking of the grapes hazardous.

Then there were women who, leaning above the stocks, exposed an opulent bosom. Some, in shorts, looked like Silvana Mangano in *Bitter Rice*. As curvy and beautiful? No, of course not. As captivating, as desirable, as deadly? Oh, far more so! Buried beneath my Christian upbringing, my latent sexuality suddenly quickened as I gathered the fruits, endowing me with incredible energy.

Page 226
A botanical illustration of a bunch of petit verdot, a historic Bordeaux vine variety that features in the assemblages of the finest *grands crus* of the Médoc.

Facing page
The Champagne harvest is a traditional affair at which the grapes are still picked by hand.

Quickly, ever more quickly: pick those grapes and get to the top of the row first, so as to help the chosen girl who would lag behind all the more readily if she could be sure of receiving assistance. Flattered, mildly mocking (the reasons for such good manners could hardly escape her), she would gaze as the young man—his back aching like hell but with unimpeachable gallantry—leapt about the stocks. She would no longer lean down, except to pluck a grape—dark, red, and fleshy—between two fingers, and burst it with her tongue.

I thought to myself, she could make an effort, and add her labors, however slow they might be, to mine—and goodness, what pleasure, what delight it would be to gather in the grapes side by side, the two of us squatting on our haunches, hidden behind the vine, as if engulfed by it, our hands brushing against one another, touching in the stocks until, with calculated inattention, we would both seize the same bunch.

On occasion two guys would turn up to lend a hand to one and the same girl. Abomination. Bad luck, however, on the one who, in a fit of pique, vacated the place to the other. The best bet was to go on as if nothing had happened, to redouble one's efforts. But without going too quickly, because it was in our interest to linger for as long as possible in her company. But even worse could happen: leaving her two lovelorn slaves to fill her pail, she would wander off to chat with another vintager, older, also a sluggard, whistling in his mustache, who would never have put himself out on her account, and with whom she would vanish between the rows.

There was always the hope one might be rewarded later on. During the dance that followed the dinner; in barns where the hay might serve as a hiding-place and mattress; among the fermentation vats, where, making a wish, expressing a desire (it is not hard to guess which), we drank, hand on heart, the first wine—lukewarm, mild, very sweet—that flowed in a stream from the press. In the Beaujolais, this raw wine is called *paradise*. It might not replace the seventh heaven, but it led to it.

The festival of the grape harvest is age-old. But mechanization, the internationalization of labor, and the more codified, more supervised interactions between the owner and vintagers, have replaced the anarchic troop of relations, friends, neighbors, students, and regulars (who would over time enter the category of friends) and today make the grape harvest less folksy, less festive.

Bacchus now has to pay Social Security dues, and demands profitability.

In former times, wassails were never down-in-the-mouth affairs, even in wartime. Colette writes of how, in 1917, one of her female friends balked at the idea of going to pick grapes in the Corrèze in a vineyard owned by Robert de Jouvenel (*Paysages et Portraits*) (Landscapes and Portraits). As she saw it, the *vendanges* were a pleasure jaunt and this meant partaking of a "rather loose freedom, of songs and dances, all raunchy language and too much food." This pleasure, this freedom she found incompatible with war. "But what can one do?" Colette answered her. "No means has yet been found of picking grapes apart from the *vendanges*."

Paradise regained. It's called the *cuvier*, the *cuverie*: in Beaujolais, the *cuvage*. It is there, in the fermenting room, where wine is made, that the changes of the last few decades have proved the most radical. There's the shift from wood to stainless steel, from pipes every which way to thermoregulation, from the mechanical to the electronically controlled winepress, from ad hoc winemaking after a glass, to enology. Even if they may appear sometimes too constricting or artificial (the addition of yeast, for example, is ironically described by Guy Renvoisé as a "medical intervention"), science and technology have appreciably improved the process, and therefore the wine. Progress has been undeniable, spectacular, particularly in the vineyards one might have once called, in an analogy with social planning policy, "disadvantaged." But this revolution has put paid to a lot of the fun. The wine room is no longer a place in which big muscles with big mouths, barechested and wearing shorts or even boxer shorts, or with their pant legs rolled up above the knees, stamped on the crop, all the while swapping risqué stories and salacious jokes with an audience of admiring females. Still, among the sugary odors of maceration, fermentation, decomposition, of volatile alcohol, it was this warmth—intimate, tacky, made up of man and grape; the skin of the one rubbing against the skin of the other—that made an evening spent pressing the crop a bawdy, carnal, or, at the very least, sensual event. The wine ran ruby red, coming to a halt with a hue of garnet, almost black. Sweet wine, syrup. It was in the winemaking room that I first heard someone utter the word "aphrodisiac."

Pages 230–31
In Alsace the grape harvest begins in September. This photograph dating from the 1970s shows harvesters snipping bunches of grapes.

Facing page
Harvesters are divided into pickers and carriers, as here in the vines of Meursault, in Burgundy.

Grape-picking

A certain boredom follows me everywhere
and I only forget my chagrin occasionally:
when I have a drink.
Also, I loved wine; I still love it.

Paul Cézanne, in a letter to Émile Zola

Facing page *Man with a Wine Glass*, c. 1918, by Amedeo Modigliani.

Veuve Clicquot

Veuve Clicquot—Widow Clicquot—has always seemed to me the stuff of dreams. She was only twenty-seven years old when François Clicquot died. Free, so young, and, lying beneath her feet, cellars brimming with thousands of bottles of champagne: by Bacchus, what a splendid catch! No man, however, ever managed to nab her. She preferred a businesswoman's independence to a second marriage. Her success was all the more extraordinary as it began a long time ago, at the beginning of the nineteenth century, and she had to impose her authority over the family of her late husband, as well as on the men in the winemaking room and in the trade. She became so skilled at it that she was dubbed "the *grande dame* of Champagne."

Do we know what François Clicquot actually died of? Yes, of a trivial fever. So trivial that the doctors didn't worry about it. In a hurry to reign over her bubbly empire, might the sparkling Mme Clicquot not have invented, to accompany her husband's desserts, a champagne-arsenic cocktail? I fantasize, picturing it in my mind's eye... if only because Veuve Clicquot is certainly worth it!

Late in life, La Veuve resembled Queen Victoria. But what about when she was young? Was she, tiddly on champagne, a "merry widow"? Was she besieged by Cock-Clicquots? Or was she better by the logbook than in a bustle, a kind of austere Dom Pérignon in petticoats? According to the testimony of her contemporaries, if she indulged her son-in-law, the brilliant though expensive-to-run Louis de Chevigné, her character was otherwise firm, decisive, and economical. If she expressed a spirit of adventure and audacity, it was exclusively in her role as a businesswoman determined to conquer the market.

Unfairly, she is never mentioned in those lists of famous women, but the name Clicquot is on (almost) everyone's lips. The Prix Veuve Clicquot is an annual award for businesswomen. The winner doesn't have to be a widow, though.

Facing page
Barbe Nicole Ponsardin-Clicquot, the *grande dame* of Champagne, who was eighty-three when Léon Cogniet painted this portrait.

And if we sip
the wine, we find
dreams coming
upon us / Out of
the imminent night.

D. H. Lawrence, "Grapes"

Château d'Yquem

I'm on the telephone and someone tells me that the members of the Academy of Wine have read and enjoyed my report, published in *Le Figaro littéraire*, on the grape harvest in Beaujolais (see "Grape-picking") and that the Marquis de Lur Saluces, its president, has invited me to its next dinner. This took place at the Relais at the Gare de l'Est in Paris, a restaurant of repute with two Michelin stars at that time. The Academy of Wine was—indeed is, since it remains active and influential—made up of proprietor-collectors of AOCs, great names from all the wine regions (and today, chefs and specialized journalists). One of its former presidents was the Marquis d'Angerville, whose Volnays were in keeping with his elegant and subtle personality. I first heard the name Lur Saluces in 1959. The family dated back to the sixteenth century. They owned a château, d'Yquem, that produced a unique wine, rare and expensive. Neither I, nor anyone in my immediate circle had ever tasted, or even had cognizance of, a bottle. And here I was, personally invited by Marquis Bertrand de Lur Saluces, master of a property, of a wine, and of a legend that could hardly be more remote from the plebeian vineyard whose *vendanges* I'd described in my article. To my twenty-four-year-old eyes, the members of the Academy of Wine appeared ancient. I felt rather left out among these people who—however delightful and attentive they were to me, the marquis in particular—seemed so erudite, so perfectly at ease identifying what they had in their plates or their glasses, and who then proceeded seamlessly to make mocking, anxious, or positive remarks on the policies of General de Gaulle. My only abiding memory is that I drank some Château d'Yquem. The taste was strange, delicious, voluptuous, insane. I was hypnotized, bamboozled. Did that really still belong to the genus *wine*? I wondered. It certainly had nothing to do with my parents' Monbazillac, which I otherwise liked. Perhaps the presence and explanations of the Marquis de Lur Saluces, the prestige of the Academy, the competence of the guests, the high spirits at the end of the meal, had all amplified my enthusiasm? And was I in a place where I could simply savor the wine—but no more, and not feel obliged to lift my eyes to heaven like a virgin after her discovery of sexual differentiation?

Page 238
The bottoms of these bottles of Sauternes form a wall of pure gold.

Facing page
Yquem is a wine that enjoys a long life. Its color darkens over time, passing from straw yellow to a dusky gold with hints of amber and caramel, and on to a translucent mahogany.

Facing page
An Yquem can flourish for twenty, fifty, a hundred years or more. This photograph shows the bottom of a nineteenth-century handblown glass bottle.

In my memory it remains the most glorious Yquem I have ever imbibed. Because it was the first (as a carefree, featherbrained young man, I did not, unfortunately, make a note of its year). Some others tasted over the following half-century, in all likelihood superior to it ('59, '70, '71, among others), do not exhale such an emotional charge. Specialists even whisper that Count Alexandre de Lur Saluces, who succeeded the marquis, has proved even more rigorous and demanding than his predecessor in further improving the quality and the renown of Yquem. But that makes no difference: no bottle of any vintage could ever compete with the undated Yquem with which I was "baptized."

Rereading these lines, I wonder whether I do not overstate the case for Yquem. It is the wine that perhaps stirs up more hyperbole, panegyric, and flights of lyricism than any other. Les Chartrons allege that "it is the extravagance of perfection." In *La Raison gourmande*, Michel Onfray evokes his first Yquem (1979), his "initiation" into the "cult" by Denis Mollat, a publisher and bookseller from Bordeaux. The philosopher is in seventh heaven: "Its shimmering colors still dance in my soul."

This "nectar" makes Frédéric Dard (who prefaced Richard Olney's book *Yquem* and who also writes hard-boiled novels) go all soft round the edges: "Yquem is our gustative faculties exalted to the inexpressible. Absolute mellowness. Complete ecstasy.... For Yquem is also light. Light you can drink." Blimey! Jean-Claude Carrière is practically levitating: "Yquem is a star, like Greta Garbo. Yquem is a model, a sort of extreme limit, an ideal horizon, which marks out and lights the road, and which shows that, at least, this one masterpiece was possible" (*Pour Yquem*). Crikey!

In the same anthology, Bernard Clavel tells a story that would deserve to appear in any handbook on French wine or on French history. "One day, having invited us to dinner with the former Prime Minister of Canada, Pierre Eliott Trudeau, and some of his friends, Alexandre de Lur Saluces presented us with a Château d'Yquem 1945. It is the best thing I have ever drunk in my life. Our host explained that he had chosen this magnum in commemoration of the Canadians who had died on our beaches to liberate us. At the end of the meal, I took Alexandre to one side and muttered to him: 'Really, you go too far! D-Day wasn't in '45, but in '44!' He shrugged his shoulders. 'I know. Unfortunately, '44 is not a great year.' It sounds like nothing, but, in the end, this reply sums it all up. Here, wine trumps even History."

I can no more think of my own life without thinking of wine and wines… than I can remember living before I breathed.

M. F. K. Fisher

Zinc

The French word *troquet* has come back into fashion. A relaxed "local," it's where workmen (or Georges Brassens, the singer-songwriter and poet, or Jacques Prévert, the poet and screenwriter) would traditionally repair to for a diminutive glass of white wine in the morning—the *p'tit blanc*—or else for something more substantial after a day's toil (or poetry): *un ballon de rouge*. The term *zinc* (from when the actual bar was often made of the gleaming metal) has now become by synecdoche a rather flashy word for a little bistro, a street-corner café, a *troquet*.

In such establishments "one for the road?" is just a rhetorical question. No one leaves *sur une seule jambe* ("on one leg"): several rounds are necessary. When a glass stands forlornly empty, the cry might go up: "You can see the gravel at the bottom of mine!" or "The little 'uns need dressing!" And so a refill arrives.

Reeking of nineteenth-century Bohemia, a *guinguette* is similar to a *troquet*, but bathed in chlorophyll, as it stands in the open air, most often next to water. It is there that Pierre-Auguste Renoir painted his amorous youths in boaters and pretty girls in summer hats, downing a lunch with several bottles in *Luncheon of the Boating Party* (1880–81): most of the glasses are empty; one young women sips at her drink. Some grapes stand in a dish. It is a fine September day.

I adore Robert Doisneau's photo of Jacques Prévert sitting alone on a café terrace on boulevard de l'Hôpital, in Paris. In front of the poet stands a café table with a glass of red. He seems to have all the time in the world. With that inevitable cigarette hanging from his lips, his poodle at his feet, he ponders. The *patron* of the bistro Le Saint-Pourçain at Saint-Sulpice—as soon as you take your seat they bring you a goodly glass of white Saint-Pourçain—informs us that the wine in Prévert's glass is a Côtes-du-Rhône.

Cheers!

Page 244
"Standing before the counter of zinc/As ten o'clock strikes/A great big plumber zinc-worker/In his Sunday best (though it's Monday)/Sings away to himself." The sheet of zinc that covers the counters in many French bars is the inspiration for "Et la fête continue" by poet Jacques Prévert.

Facing page
Jacques Prévert at a Pedestal Table, photographed by Robert Doisneau in Paris, 1955.

Pages 248–49
Renoir's *Luncheon of the Boating Party* was painted on the terrace of the Maison Fournaise, a *guinguette* in Chatou that is still worth visiting for a glass or two.

249

Zinc

Credits

Photographic Credits

The publisher has endeavored to contact copyright holders and obtain their permission for the use of copyright material. In the event of any error or omission, the publisher would be grateful if notified, and will rectify any inadvertent omissions in future printings.

p. 2 © Cyril le Tourneur d'Ison
p. 4 © Paul Avoine
p. 6 © BPK, Berlin, Dist. RMN-Grand Palais/Elke Walford
p. 10 © Succession Picasso, 2013, RMN-Grand Palais/Hervé Lewandowski
p. 12 © Centre Pompidou, MNAM-CCI, Dist. RMN/Adam Rzepka/ADAGP, Paris 2013
pp. 14–15 © Goteborgs Konstmuseum, Sweden/The Bridgeman Art Library
p. 17 © Jacques Guillard/Scope Image
pp. 18–19 © Cyril le Tourneur d'Ison
p. 21 © Estate Brassaï—RMN-Grand Palais/Michèle Bellot
pp. 22–23 © BKP Berlin, Dist. RMN-Grand Palais/image BStGS
p. 24 © Christian Sarramon
p. 26 © Ferdinando Scianna/Magnum Photos
p. 29 © Archives Alinari, Florence Dist. RMN-Grand Palais/Nicolas Larusso
pp. 30–31 © Giraudon/The Bridgeman Art Library
p. 32 © Collection Jean-Baptiste Leroux/Château de Versailles, Dist. RMN-Grand Palais/J.-B. Leroux
p. 35 © Musée national d'histoire et d'art de Luxembourg, photo: MNHA/Tom Lucas
p. 36 © Pierre Cottin
p. 39 © Hameau Duboeuf
pp. 40–41 © Agnès Pivot
p. 42 © Micheline Pelletier/Sygma/Corbis
p. 43 © Gallimard
pp. 44–45 © Jean-Luc Barde/Scope Images
p. 47 © Giraudon/The Bridgeman Art Library/© Rhoner/ADAGP, Paris 2013
p. 49 © Michel Guillard/Scope Image
pp. 50–51 © Michel Guillard/Scope Image
pp. 52–53 © Guillaume de Laubier
p. 54 © Charles Martin, The Stapleton Collection/The Bridgeman Art Library
p. 57 © Hameau Duboeuf
p. 58 © Christian Sarramon
pp. 60–61 © Henri Cartier-Bresson/Magnum Photos
p. 63 © Owen Franken/Corbis
p. 64 © Sophie Bassouls/Corbis
p. 66 © Spaarnestad/Rue des Archives
p. 69 All rights reserved
p. 70 © Guillaume de Laubier
pp. 72–73 © Rue des Archives/BCA
p. 75 © Mouron.Cassandre. Lic 2013-25-05-03 www.cassandre.fr
p. 77 © Ramen // Photocuisine
p. 78 © Philip Reynaers/Photonews/Gamma
p. 81 © akg-images
pp. 82–83 © David Hurn/Magnum Photos
p. 84 © Michel Guillard/Scope Image
p. 87 © Sudres // Photocuisine
p. 88 © Jacques Guillard/Scope Image
p. 91 © Cyril le Tourneur d'Ison
p. 92 © Christian Sarramon
p. 94 © Succession Marcel Duchamp/ADAGP, Paris 2013, © Centre Pompidou, MNAM-CCI, Dist. RMN-Grand Palais/All rights reserved
p. 97 © Alberto Bali/Willi's Wine Bar—Detail of the first contemporary poster by Alberto Bali, made in 1984 for Willi's Bottle Art Collection, reproduced here with the gracious permission of Alberto Bali & Willi's Wine Bar
p. 98 © Gueorgui Pinkhassov/Magnum Photos
p. 101 © Charles Martin, The Stapleton Collection/The Bridgeman Art Library
p. 103 © Mouron.Cassandre. Lic 2013-25-05-03 www.cassandre.fr
pp. 104–5 © RMN-Grand Palais (Musée du Louvre)/All rights reserved
p. 107 © Giraudon/The Bridgeman Art Library
p. 108 All rights reserved
p. 110 © Christian Sarramon
p. 113 All rights reserved
p. 115 © Hameau Duboeuf
p. 116 © Camille Moirenc, domaine Canarelli
p. 119 © Cyril le Tourneur d'Ison
p. 120 © akg-images/Paul Almasy
p. 122 © The Metropolitan Museum of Art, Dist. RMN-Grand Palais/image of the MMA
p. 125 © Cyril le Tourneur d'Ison
pp. 126–27 © RMN-Grand Palais (Musée du Louvre)/Michèle Bellot
p. 129 © BPK, Berlin, Dist. RMN-Grand Palais/Elke Estel/Hans Peter Kluth
pp. 130–31 © Marcel Dole/Rue des Archives

p. 132 © Caulfield, Patrick (1936–2005)/Imperial College Healthcare Charity Art Collection, London/The Bridgeman Art Library/ADAGP, Paris 2013
p. 135 © Michel Labelle
p. 136 © Jacques Guillard/Scope Image
pp. 138–39 © Paul Palau
p. 141 © Jacques Guillard/Scope Image
p. 142 © Richard Haughton
p. 144 © Ian Berry/Magnum Photos
p. 146–47 © Jacques Guillard/Scope Image
p. 148 © RMN-Grand Palais (Musée du Louvre)/Hervé Lewandowski
pp. 150–51 © akg-images/Electa
p. 153 © Hameau Duboeuf
p. 155 © Christian Sarramon
p. 156 © Selva/Leemage
p. 159 © Mary Evans/Rue des Archives
pp. 160–61 © Mary Evans/Rue des Archives
p. 162 © C. Devleeschauwer
p. 164 © Peter Turnley/Rapho
p. 167 © Dupuy-Berberian
p. 168 © Massimo Merlini/Gettyimages
p. 170 © Philippe Martineau
p. 173 © Cuboimages/Scope Image
p. 174 © Guillaume de Laubier
p. 176 © Beatriz Orduña/Gettyimages
p. 178 © Superstock/Rue des Archives
pp. 180–81 © Christian Guy/Hemis.fr
p. 182 © Jean Carlu/ADAGP, Paris/Christian Sarramon
p. 183 © Cyril le Tourneur d'Ison
p. 185 © Voutch/voutch.com
p. 186 © Jacques Guillard/Scope Image
pp. 188–89 © Jacques Guillard/Scope Image
pp. 190–91 © Jacques Guillard/Scope Image
p. 192 © akg-images/Rabatti – Domingie
p. 194 © Elliott Erwitt/Magnum Photos
p. 197 © Ghislaine Bavoillot
p. 198 © RMN-Grand Palais (Musée du Louvre)/Gérard Blot
p. 201 © Cluzel // Photocuisine
p. 203 © Michel Tolmer
pp. 204–5 © Karl Lagerfeld
p. 206 © Peter Willi/The Bridgeman Art Library
p. 209 © Stapleton Collection/Corbis
p. 210 © Stefania Mizara/Corbis
p. 212 © YinYang/Gettyimages
p. 215 © Jean-Louis Bernuy
pp. 216–17 © Jean-Louis Bernuy
p. 218 © Mary Evans/Rue des Archives
p. 221 © Cyril le Tourneur d'Ison
p. 222 © Cyril le Tourneur d'Ison
p. 225 © Guillaume de Laubier
p. 226 © DeAgostini/Leemage
p. 229 © Peter Marlow/Magnum Photos
pp. 230–31 © Bruno Barbey/Magnum Photos
p. 233 © Ferdinando Scianna/Magnum Photos
p. 235 © Modigliani, Jesi Collection, Milan, Italy/The Bridgeman Art Library
p. 236 © Domaine Veuve Clicquot
p. 238 © Cyril le Tourneur d'Ison
p. 241 © Christian Sarramon
p. 242 © Christian Sarramon
p. 244 © Ferdinando Scianna/Magnum Photos
p. 246 © Robert Doisneau/Rapho
pp. 248–49 © Corbis
p. 252 © Henri Cartier-Bresson/Magnum Photos
p. 253 © Plon/Alain Bouldouyre
pp. 254–55 © Rue des Archives/AGIP

Front cover and spine (top): © YinYang / Gettyimages
Spine (bottom): © Hameau Duboeuf
Back cover, from top left:
© Jacques Guillard / Scope Image; © Estate Brassaï – RMN-Grand Palais / Michèle Bellot; © Superstock / Rue des Archives; © Hameau Duboeuf; © Pierre Cottin; © Henri Cartier-Bresson / Magnum Photos
Portrait on flap: © Patrick Othoniel / JDD

Quotation on page 11: from Robert Mondavi, *Harvests of Joy: How the Good Life Became Great Business*, published by Harcourt Brace & Company, First Harvest edition, 1999. Copyright © 1998 by Robert Mondavi.

Quotation on page 117: from Jay McInerney, *A Hedonist in the Cellar: Adventures in Wine*, published by Alfred A. Knopf, 2006. Copyright © 2006 by Bright Lights, Big City, Inc.

Quotation on page 124: from Richard Olney, *Lulu's Provençal Table*, published by HarperCollins Publishers, 1994. Copyright © 1994 by Richard Olney.

Quotation on page 137: from Jim Harrison, "Wine," in *Adventures in Wine: True Stories of Vineyards and Vintages around the World*, ed. Thom Elkjer, published by Travelers' Tales, 2002. Copyright © 2002 Travelers' Tales, Inc.

Quotation on page 169: from Paulo Coelho, *Brida: A Novel*, published by HarperCollins Publishers, 2008. Copyright © 2008 by Paulo Coelho; English translation © 2008 by Margaret Jull Costa.

Poster reproduced with the gracious permission of Alberto Bali and Willi's Wine Bar.

Acknowledgments

The author wishes to thank Anne-Marie Bourgnon
and Agnès Pivot.

The editor thanks all those who contributed to the image selection for this book,
and gives special thanks to Bertrand Auboyneau, Alberto Bali,
Charles Berberian, Sylvain Boivert, Alain Bouldouyre, Georges Duboeuf,
Franck Duboeuf, Philippe Dupuy, Karl Lagerfeld, Caroline Lebar, Agnès Pivot,
Mark Williamson, and Jonathan Zlatics.

Facing page   *Winegrower in Champagne,* by Henri Cartier-Bresson, 1960.
Pages 254–55   Paul Bocuse showing Bernard Pivot the Beaujolais bearing
a special label by Georges Duboeuf; it was bottled specially for the party
following the last broadcast of *Apostrophes* (June 22, 1990).

This book is an abridged and illustrated edition of the original work
published in French by Éditions Plon in 2006.

Editorial Director: Ghislaine Bavoillot
Original Layout Design: Isabelle Ducat
Translated from the French by David Radzinowicz
Copyediting: Penelope Isaac
Layout Adaptation and Typesetting: Gravemaker+Scott
Proofreading: Helen Downey
Color Separation: IGS, France
Printed in Singapore by Tien Wah Press

Originally published in French as *Dictionnaire amoureux du vin, version illustrée*
© Plon & Flammarion, S.A., Paris, 2013

English-language edition
© Plon & Flammarion, S.A., Paris, 2014

All rights reserved.
No part of this publication may be reproduced in any form or by any means, electronic,
photocopy, information retrieval system, or otherwise, without written permission from
Flammarion, S.A.
87, quai Panhard et Levassor
75647 Paris Cedex 13

editions.flammarion.com

14 15 16   3 2 1

ISBN: 978-2-08-020154-6

Dépôt légal: 02/2014

... Saint-Julien · Banyuls · ...
... Régnié · Bourgogne · Bourgueil · Mus...
...nt-Estèphe · Côte-de-Brouilly · Beaune · ...
... Pommard · Rivesaltes · Collioure · Alox...
...née-Conti · Morgon · Champagne · Côte...
...lin-à-Vent · Pinot Noir · Yquem · Bordela...
...sling · Sylvaner · Tokay · Chassagne-Mo...
...olle-Musigny · Nuits-Saint-Georges · Châ...
... Boyd-Cantenac · Cabernet Sauvignon · ...
...-de-Serrant · Chénas · Chasselas · Mau...
... Puligny-Montrachet · Monthélie · Vosn...
...-Clos-de-Bèze · Frontignan · Quincy · Reu...
... Bonnes Mares · Chambertin · Châteaune...
... Meursault · Sauternes · Côtes du Rhôn...
...Côtes de Duras · Beaujolais · Volnay ·...
...ougeot · Pouilly-Fuissé · Château Margau...
... Vouvray · Médoc · Saint-Amour · Ro...
... Chardonnay · Haut-Brion · Pétrus · M...
...teau Lagrange · Mouton Rothschild · Rie...

...ambertin · Châteauneuf-du-Pape · Sau...
...auternes · Côtes du Rhône · Régnié · Bour...
...eaujolais · Volnay · Saint-Estèphe · Côte...
...uissé · Château Margaux · Pommard · Rive...
...oc · Saint-Amour · Romanée-Conti · Morgo...
...aut-Brion · Pétrus · Moulin-à-Vent · Pinot...
...outon Rothschild · Riesling · Sylvaner ·...
...ertin · Juliénas · Chambolle-Musigny · Nu...
...âconnais · Saint-Véran · Boyd-Cantenac ·...
...aux du Layon · Coulée-de-Serrant · Ché...
...raves · Côte Chalonnaise · Puligny-Montra...
...hiroubles · Chambertin-Clos-de-Bèze · Fro...
...nay · Brouilly · Fleurie · Bonnes Mares · ...
...Banyuls · Saint-Émilion · Meursault · Sau...
...ourgueil · Muscadet · Côtes de Duras ·...
...rouilly · Beaune · Clos Vougeot · Pouilly-F...
...Collioure · Aloxe-Corton · Vouvray · Méd...
...hampagne · Côte de Nuits · Chardonnay ·...
...Yquem · Bordelais · Château Lagrange · M...